P9-CMP-694

ROMAN BARTHOLOW

ROMAN BARTHOLOW

BY

EDWIN ARLINGTON ROBINSON

New York
THE MACMILLAN COMPANY
1923

To
PERCY MACKAYE

ROMAN BARTHOLOW

ROMAN BARTHOLOW

I

WHERE now the morning light of a new spring
    Fell warm on winter, patient in his grave,
And on a world not patient, Bartholow—
Like one above a dungeon where for years
Body and soul had fought futility
In vain for their deliverance—looked away
Over the falling lawn that was alive
And green again between him and the river.
Steel-blue below him, through a yellow dusk
Of trees, he saw the flowing gleam of water,
Whereon his fancy limned the mirrored face
Of spring, too blind again with her own beauty
To measure man's advantage,—though he might
This morning have addressed a votive shout,

Affirming his emergence, to the Power
That filled him as light fills a buried room
When earth is lifted and the sun comes in.

He would have raised an altar now to spring,
And one to God; and one more to the friend
Who, coming strangely out of the unknown
To find him here in his ancestral prison,
Had brought with him release. Never before
Would he have said that any friend alive
Had magic to make light so gross a weight
As long had held him frozen out of sense
And hearing of all save a dead negation
That would not let him die. When Gabrielle,
Serving a triple need, so fondly sought
And rarely found, of beauty, mind and fire,
Had failed him—where was life, and what was left?
So Bartholow had asked himself in vain,
And many a time again without an answer;
While she, in her discreet bewilderment,
Had known him only as a furniture
That was alive and tiresome, he supposed,
And only rather bravely to be cherished,

Like a mute fretful changeling; for the soul,
At last insurgent in him, she knew not.
"Our souls are foreign in us till our fears
Attest them and they clamor to be known
And owned; they are our slayers and our saviours,
And we more slain than saved."   So Bartholow
Had reasoned once; and so, for all he knew
Might have abandoned reason to the ruin
Of all the joy regained that was within him
And in the morning light that was around him,
And over this old ivied house of stone,
Built years ago by one whose glowering faith
In gold on earth and hope of it in heaven
Hung where the shadows of a century
Had favored his ancestral eminence.

Penn-Raven, on his first observing him
Dim-featured on the wall, had said at last,
Slowly, "If there is much of him in you,
Your soul had better never been aroused.
Now show me your grandmother, if you please,
And then your mother.   Never mind the rest,
For you are not the son of any father."

[3]

Bartholow, delving then where memory
Found love at odds with umbrage, had essayed
A patent laugh. "But you are right," he said;
"My father was to me a mighty stranger—
Fearsome, but always on the side of right
As he discerned it. There were some collisions
Between us, and a few sparks, though no fire
That ever burned enough to make a scar.
For the most part he let me go my way;
And when the way was hard, I made it so.
We'll say that many are better and some worse
Than I was then." Penn-Raven, being a stranger
In those days, had said little; Bartholow
Said not much more. Each knew the other's heart,
Or so he fancied, and had found it right.
Later Penn-Raven, having found the soul
In Bartholow that ailed him, had with ease
Ineffable healed it—having wrought meanwhile
More than his indeterminate attention
Saw waiting for his pains. More than a year
A neighbor, and of late, unwillingly,
A resident saviour domiciled, he had lived
More as an over-lord than as a guest,

Entreating always, always amiably,
A day not far off on the calendar
To mark the festival of his departure.
There would be always locusts and wild honey
Enough somewhere.   So that for gratitude,
Bartholow loved him almost as a novice
Loves God, though not remembering there are faces
On which one may not wholly look and live.

But now, with all this morning light upon him
He looked about him with a life renewed
Upon a world renewed, and gave himself
Less to remembering an obscure monition
Than to confessing an assured renascence,—
Albeit his whim was once or twice to fancy
That if he stamped upon the footworn flags
Beneath him, he should hear a sullen ring
Of buried emptiness, like that wherein
His endless and indignant yesterdays
Had held him.   He was holding a long breath
Of living air, for joy of having it,
When suddenly a footfall and a voice
Summoned his eyes agreeably to the sight

Of one whose garment of mortality,
Fashioned unhandsomely of misfit patchwork,
Was made for him to wear, not asking why.
Bartholow, smiling, looked him up and down
Aware that in his gaze was no encroaching
On more than wilful incongruity,
Flaunting a more pernicious taste in frenzy
Than order would elect.   Soiled heavy shoes
Laced half way to the knee, were to the purpose;
The rest was all a chequered inflammation
Of myriad hues that had, like those on Joseph,
No capturable names.   A fishing basket
Hung weighted from one shoulder, and a rod,
Held with a flexile and immaculate hand
Lay wrapped across the other; and underneath
A shapeless variegated sort of cap
There was a face made more for comedy
Than for the pain that comedy concealed,
Socratic, unforgettable, grotesque,
Inscrutable, and alone.   Bartholow gave
His hand in greeting to this apparition,
Who searched him in his turn as if in doubt.

"Good morning, sir, my name is Umfraville;
But I'll eat fire and smoke if I know yours.
I make it at a venture sixty.days
Or more ago that I found hereabouts
A restive and unpleasant lord of acres
Who had unhappily no joy of me
Or pleasure of himself.   So, naturally,
I vanished, knowing there were dogs about,
And weapons.   He was wan and rather dour
To look on, and his eyes were like two lamps
Preparing to go out.   The name of him
Was Roman Bartholow—somewhat a scholar,
Somewhat a farmer in a parlor way,
And something of a delver in the dark,
Hoping to find there his immortal soul.
He never said it in so many words,
But that's the esoteric upshot of it.
I knew him once when even the sight of him
Was anodyne for sorrow or disaster,
And when his feet had wings.   He wore a look
In those days more or less akin to yours
Today, but you are not the man.   Where is he?
And who is this who does me now the honor

Of giving me his honorable hand?
O saepe mecum, here be trout for breakfast,
If you expound. If not, away we go,
The fishes and the fisherman together,
Never again for you to contemplate.
Meanwhile, appraise them; and if they invoke
Approval, pay for them as heretofore;
For I have brought with me an evil thirst
That barks away from water."

                              Bartholow,
With cordial and explicit gratitude,
Obeyed; and when the empty creel returned,
More followed on a tray. "No, not for me,"
He said. "The morning is itself enough—
For me."

   "Then by my soul," said Umfraville,
"You have found yours. No doubt, some day or other,
I shall find mine, but not by fishing for it.
Once I believed that I had found my soul,
But therein I was wrong and only bilious.
We cannot harvest evidence unseen

As we do carrots, and we cannot buy it;
Nor may we take it from the open hand
Of love or friendship, merely wishing it.
Otherwise, maybe we should not be here,
Toiling so mortal hard, or not so hard,
To stay a little longer.   You and I,
As I conceive, are not among the toilers—
Though God send I may give you no offense
Or give my tongue a too familiar motion;
For you are on the broad and open road
Where all your friends and enemies are with you,
Impinging on your equanimity
Each in his way, and you in turn observing
How much of easy death in life there is
Where life is easy.   I, who have neither friend—
Save you—nor enemy worth mentioning,
Go as I will, or as I must, by ways
Not on the map; and that's as well for me.
By which you mark that I'll be serious
When instigated by a miracle.
In brief, what lost elixir have you swallowed,
And when am I to know the taste of it?"

Bartholow saw the spirit on the tray
Diminishing, and answered, "I've a doubt
If your interior machinery
Has need of an elixir more remote
Than you have here.   For you there is no age.
Another forty years will find you young,
Still eating Greek and Latin, and, as now,
Still fishing—not for man or for your soul,
But for the only joy there is for you
That lives in water.   There's a difference
In one who lives to see himself behind him,
And after a few years of living death
Sees a new self before him, as I do.
There was a friend who came to make it so,
And one that if I gave him all I own
Would leave me rich in wealth unpayable.
How much of all this do you understand?"

"I understand a fraction more of it,
Maybe, than you have told; for I'm a reader,
And there are books that walk.   I know your friend,
Though only as a motion on the landscape,
Out of my world.   If he has made you over,
If he has raised the veil and given you eyes

To see what's going on where I see nothing,
Well, I say peace be with him, and with you.
I am not worthy of your mysteries—
If you remember all that a man should
Of Aristophanes."
                         "Which I do not,"
Bartholow said, smiling. "But you are worthy
Of all the mysteries of earth and heaven
That your content may cry for. Casually,
What surety have you that your world and his
Are all so different as you see them now?
How is it, if you know the gentleman
Only outside, you are so sure of him?"

"I may have known a gentleman or so,
Or so I tell myself," said Umfraville,
"But I should look a little at my shoes,
Or maybe at the stars, before I tossed
A name too soon to one that raised the veil,
Merely because he raised it. Being myself
A nondescript, I take upon myself
A more ingenuous right of utterance
Than tongues of others ordinarily

Might sanction or employ.   What matters it,
When there be some of God's elect who make
A warfare of a sirloin?   Observation
Might, with a misconceived authority,
Fill hell with saints, and set the devil on high
To frustrate the archangels.   What's it all
To me, one way or other?   Born with a face
That on a bullfrog would ensure for life
The lucubrations of a celibate,
I ask, in God's name, what's it all to me?
I see that you are noticing my raiment,
And murmuring, *Kyrie eleison*,—
Greek for What Next.   I notice it myself.
I must have color without, if none within;
Though never of a hue so violent
As to fill fish with terror when I seek
Their innocent and iridescent lives
Whereon we lower than the angels feed.
Now I'll go home again across the river,
While yet your Caledonian poison plays
And sings within me, not unpleasantly;
And if perchance in some unlikely future
You find yourself astray and in the dark,

And the veil down again, and if you ask
What fellow it was one morning in the spring
Who said that of all men he found in you
Alone a friend, and would, were it feasible,
Pay with an arm to prove his loyalty,—
I'll tell you, truly as I know this hand
Of yours that I am holding now in mine,
The appointed words that are for you to say:
Say it was one who laughed when others laughed
And thereby kept a sorry craft afloat
That else had foundered or been strangely missing;
Say it was nature's inadvertency
Confessed in one on whom there were few men,
And fewer women, to look humanly,
And one that only dogs could ever love;
Say it was one who lived again the past
In books, where there were none to laugh at him,
And where—to him, at least—a world was kind
That is no more a world.   More frugally,
Say it was Umfraville, the fisherman."

Bartholow, still retaining the warm hand
In his, met now the flushed impossible face

Before him with a sorrow at his heart
And a smile on his lips: "I will say all
You tell me, or as much as I remember.
You hardly ask of me that I shall call you
All the quaint names that you have called yourself.
Out of another mouth you might resent them
And ask what their involved irrelevance
Might intimate.   All the same, I'll not forget
The name that's yours.   Be sure of that.   Good-bye!
One of these days I'll find myself across
The river, at your door—if you invite me—
And weigh the tonnage of my ignorance
Upon your classic scales."

                              The visitor
Made answer only with a warmer clasp
And a long gaze of misty gratefulness.
Then he went slowly on his way alone,
As he went everywhere, and out of sight—
Leaving his friend reborn to breathe again,
Insatiably, the morning of new life.

II

AT last, having inhaled the morning air
    Until it made him ache with renovation,
He gazed again below him at the river
Where now another face was dimly mirrored.
The learned fisherman, who knew books and brooks
Alike, surely had not the face of spring,
Yet for the moment his uncouth regard
Supplanted nature; and while Bartholow
Stood watching the cool water through the trees,
An airy caricature of loneliness
Hovered a while between him and all else.
Then, with a sigh for such a piece of life
So doomed and irremediably defeated,
He walked away over the footworn flags
And over a long driveway of new gravel,
Circuitously through acres of young grass
To the old iron gate, set long ago

By the same ancestor in whom Penn-Raven
Saw for his host no lineal obligation.

By this time Bartholow pursued again
A phantom fisherman that was alive
Somewhere alone between him and the town,
And in his dim pursuit he found himself
Considering the oblique and infinite
Amend awaiting many before they leave
A world where Fate, as for the sport of it,
Might once have reared invisible walls whereover
No crippled atomy should ever climb.
"Meanwhile," he thought, "it might be worse, and isn't;
He has a pittance, and so cannot starve;
And he wants little, having little need
Of more than he would use. That's how it is
We salve ourselves with our complacency,
And edge our morning appetite for trout,
Which others not so favored bring to us
Because they love us. And if that be so,
We'll honor them at least with our attention
To theirs. He must have caught me with his hook
This morning, for I feel a string that holds me.

In such a world as this no creature born
Should have to lose it for a face like that."
Still pondering, and with a rueful shrug
Of helplessness, he turned about and walked
The winding gravel to his house again
And entered it—first having filled himself
Gratefully with a final inhalation,
Like one forestalling a robust illusion
That after breakfast there would be no air.

Inside again, he smiled as he remembered
The startled fisherman's inquiring look
Of incredulity on his approach
With his moist offering, and went upstairs
To find if in a mirror there should live
Sufficient warrant of another's wonder;
And there, before the reassuring glass,
He found a face at least agreeable,
And surely not the blank and haggard mask
That he had seen so long there in the dark
Of his devouring fear and hopelessness,
When hope was a lost word and happiness
Not even a ghost that haunted him. He saw

[17]

Before him now a man of middle height,
Shaped well for life and for the exercise
Of any task that he saw facing him—
Where, be it here confessed, he saw not any
That he might not approve in his own humor,
To ponder or perform.   A roundish head,
Of no ethereal or severe distinction,
Carried a face that would have passed unscanned
And unrecorded through the worldly gates
That his indifference left unvisited,
Save when his wife saw fit that he be seen
Where he saw little and remembered less.
He stood for a long time, incredulously
Intent upon the beaming duplicate
Of one who must have been, past any question,
The fond original of all he saw
To please him and to paint that happy smile
Of grateful recognition and thanksgiving;
And there he might have stayed, admiring life
In its revival, until eventide—
Had there not come, unsummoned, silently
Into the pleasant scene the mirrored grace
Of one whose laughter was no counterfeit,

And had no purpose that a man reborn
Might always in a moment wholly seize.

Gabrielle waited, laughing half aloud,
Most of her laughter coming from her eyes;
"Was ever such a morning admiration
Of anything so perfect or so happy?"
She spoke, and lingered, while he flushed a little
As he came forward slowly to the door
Where she was framed and her dark morning beauty
Was like an armor for the darts of time,
Where they fell yet for nothing and were lost
Against the magic of her slenderness.
All wrapped in garnet wool, still watching him,
And laughing with her sleepy-shining eyes,
"Was it Apollo, or Antinous,
You met there in the looking-glass?" she said.
"My classic gentlemen have lost their names,
But they were monstrous handsome, all of them,
As I know you are not. I have him now—
Narcissus; and he liked himself so much
That he is now a little vegetable,
And nothing more. You might remember that.

If I had come but half an instant later,
I should have seen you dancing at yourself.
I'm certain of it."

               He came farther forward,
And laying his warm hands upon her shoulders
Looked hungrily into her laughing eyes,
Which looked away as if the sun had hurt them.
"My soul was dancing here for joy already,
Before you came," he told her; "even as once
A king in Israel danced with all his might
Before an ark.   His wife, who didn't like it,
Saw him and laughed.   You might remember that.
David was not infallibly a pattern,
Yet he had notions that were sound enough
Concerning wives who laugh.   He sent them off
To brood alone on their discrepancies,—
And they were sorry then they ever laughed
At David when he danced."   He drew her fondly
And slowly nearer, holding up her face
To gaze upon: "You might remember that."

"And you might let me go; for I'm no more
Than half awake and only partly dry.

You might go down and look at your grandfather.
If you are not a spider, go away—
For I'm not up. For heaven's sake—!"

                         He crushed
The fragrant elements of mingled wool
And beauty in his arms and pressed with his
A cool silk mouth, which made a quick escape,
Leaving an ear—to which he told unheard
The story of his life intensively.

"I know," she answered, in a purring voice
That had somewhere a muffled hardness in it;
"And you have heard me saying without end
That I'm as glad as you that you are born
Again; for both of us were nearly gone.
With half another of those years behind us,
We should have been two moving skeletons
With just enough meat on us to scare people
Whenever we should move. I know some things,
But I'm an ignoramus of the soul,
As you two men have noticed. I've a soul,
I hope, yet I'm not sure." She looked up slowly,
And tapped his cheeks with her pink finger-tips.

"You may be seeming, in a sleepy way,
To think you do not know, or care," he said;
"But you are thinking harder of your breakfast,
And that's a normal thought. The weight your soul
Is bearing now in its obscurity
Is more that you are hungry than uncertain."

She nodded. "And I hope there's more than porridge,
For I'm as hungry as that one-eyed person
Who lived with others like him in a cave."

"The ravens have attended to all that;
And we are of the fortunate this morning,
In that we shall not starve."

                    "You mean your Raven?
What has the Raven found for us to eat?"

"No, quite another bird. A worthy one,
Though quite another, of another plumage.
Good-bye. Remember David, and repent."

He left her and went singing down the stairs,
Where presently, when she conceived herself

Secure for matutinal panegyric,
She found him scowling in the library
Over some pages that she could not read.
"What in the world are you at now, so early,"
She questioned him, "and why do you scowl so?"

He felt a flitting pressure of her lips
Upon his hair, and looked up gratefully:
"I'm at the oldest of all occupations,
Looking for something that I cannot find—
Buried alive this time in an old play.
Listen: *Einai me tōn sōn axion
Musteriōn*.   What do you make of that?"

"No more than music.   Has it any meaning?
If I could read it I should not need you
For music in the morning.   It sings well,
But you must ruin it all for my poor wits."

" 'Let me be worthy of your mysteries,'
Approximately, is the ruin of it
That your poor wits require.   Do you believe me

Worthy of yours—your mysteries?"   He gazed
Into her languid eyes inquiringly
And laughed as if in answer.

                              'I believe
That you are always foolish in the morning,"
She said.   "Shall we be waiting for the Raven,
Or shall we be at breakfast when he comes
In all his weird magnificence to greet us?
We shall not have to wait.   I hear him croaking.
Never in all my quiet life before
Was there a morning when I heard so much
Man-music in it.   He says, *Chi mi frena* . . .
And how is one to know?"

                    The minstrel checked
The flow of his irrelevant aubade
Before the doorway of the library:
"Good morning! If you heard my song, forgive me.
Like the ordained, I sing because I must.
You two should not have waited."   He came in,
Fixing on each in turn a violet eye
That smouldered, with a darker fire behind

Which kindled with an intermittent flame
A nameless light whereon but few could look
Long without flinching—Bartholow being one
Who could; which may have been, or not, a part
Of his revival into a new being
Like and unlike the old. As he surveyed
Penn-Raven coming in, the eyes he met,
Softening with a slow unconsciousness,
Took on a sheen of innocence no player
Might own among his arts. No subterfuge,
Or sleeping evil or apparent scorn
Was in their changing power. The square face
And heavy forehead were for more men's envy
Than a soft mouth, where lips that were too full
Were for the cautious like a false addition
To be deplored. The nose was large and right;
And, as men stand, Penn-Raven would have stood
Firmer to see than many who had more
Of earth to stand on. It was in his eyes
That most of him was latent or revealed
Unto the eyes of others who could find him.
And there were few who could—Bartholow being,
For price of larger sight, one who could not.

"This morning there are mysteries abroad,"
Said Gabrielle; "and even at this table
I'm warned of one awaiting us. I guess
What's coming only as I read a name
That's not yet written. Well, here it is. Be careful."

Penn-Raven's eyes, already luminous
With admiration, were now flashing on her
The shine of a new interest. "Mysteries,"
He said, "when out of place are injudicious;
But here, if I see truly, I see trout."

"Why not? You look at them for all the world
As if you were the devil's child who caught them."

"How do you know it was the devil's child
Who caught them?" Bartholow said, indulgently.
"I'll say it was a sad and learned man
Who caught them—leaving you and our friend here
To comfort him with your imagined thanks.
He has imagination."

                    "Not too much,
I hope," she murmured, with a faint recoil;

"That is, if he's the same unhappy monster
That once, a year ago, brought you a gift
Like this, and his face with it. For I've seen him
Here in this house; and he has looked at me.
Pfah! Take it away, for I'm not hungry."

Bartholow frowned. "If you had ridden your fancy
Around the last immeasurable orbit
Of the last satellite of the last sun,
You and your fancy could have trundled home
No sort of wilder trash than you imply
When you say that."

                    She broke a roll and laughed:
"Surely an avalanche of words like yours
Would crush the morning appetite of lions.
I like the man who said that all who talk
Through breakfast should have poison in their coffee.
Hereafter I'll have mine in bed again."

"By which you mean," Penn-Raven said, removing
A spinal column from the pink-white flesh
Before him on the plate, "you fear the Greeks,
Et dona ferentes. Contrariwise, I wish

There might be more of them.   Hush, my dear sir,
Or she may change her mind." He munched amain
The delicate fresh viand in his mouth,
Beaming on Bartholow and Gabrielle
With childish eyes that were as innocent
As those of a large house-dog meditating.

"I know a lady who, as I remember,
Has chattered well at breakfast before now,"
Bartholow said. He struck away the tail
Of a large trout with a malingering fork,
And eyed the rest of it indifferently.
"My notion was to hear you purr a little
Over a mild surprise; and all you do
Is to make faces and be disappointing.
I'm glad that in the past no vanity
Has ever told me that I understood
Your ways and cerebrations, for I don't.
What in the name of all trout that are speckled
Has a man's face to do with eating them?
And why, because he did your face the honor—
An easy one, I grant—of looking at it,
Must you be seeing in him only a satyr?

I will assure you now that all you saw
Was his affliction in the difference,
And a soul groping in its loneliness."

"I think the Raven wants another fish.
Let him have mine; for mine is beautiful,
Even in death," she said.

                    Penn-Raven turned,
And after an involuntary frown
That had a question in it, the keen eyes
Put off again their sharpness.   Then he said,
"Hush, hush, my children.   If you mean to fight,
I'll take the fishes off into a corner
And eat them all myself.   What man accurst
Is he who has in his inheritance
A face that shatters happiness like yours?
If he be one that I have passed in town
Sometimes, he has a face to frighten Hogarth,
But never one to keep him long away
From such a fare as this.   Dear sir, and madam,
I cannot on the fringe of decency
Consume alone the sum of everything;

Wherefore, if only out of loving-kindness,
Bartholow, eat that fish."

                    "I beg your pardon,"
He said, and that was nearly all he said
While he essayed without enthusiasm
The far-sought evidence of Umfraville's
Ill timed remembrance.   Gabrielle, insisting,
Gave hers to her expostulating guest.
"They may be large, but they're not numerous,"
She said, "and I should weep to see them wasted."

"One's ignorance would not envisage you
As overmuch at home among the weeping,"
He told her; and his eyes changed while he smiled
And studied her like one strangely in earnest.

"Not freely at the table, or not often;
Though I can weep as well as anyone
When I've a mind to."

                    "And when you've a mind to,"
Bartholow said, "you can be rational.

I'd say this morning you had lost your wits,
Only I know you haven't; though God knows
I've given you leave to lose a few of them
During some years of mine that we'll forget,
Or say that we forget, now they are gone.
On unforeseen occasions when you turn
Your bee loose in that comely skull of yours,
I may be critical, while underneath
I'm all humility and admiration."

"As I," she said, "am all acknowledgment.
Now everything is as it was before,
And we are quite the same as yesterday.
The Raven sees it, and his feathers all
Are smooth again. We startled him somewhat."

"The Raven has no comment or complaint,"
The guest assured her, "and he has no part
In your engaging fits and ebullitions,—
Although the face of one unlovely stranger
Would hardly seem enough—but I refrain.
I say no more. Both you and your good man
Are still intact; and there are birds outside

[31]

That sing mellifluously in the trees,
And the sun shines on everything. What more
Are we to ask, or likely to receive?
With your agreement I'll dismiss myself
And leave you to bind up your wounds alone.
My call is for a smoke along the river—
Your proof that I'm a creature still of earth,
Fit yet for no Nirvana. Peace be with you."

He went, and Gabrielle soon followed him
As far as to the door, where she surveyed
With tired and indolent indifference
The green beginning of another summer.
Bartholow, coming after, looked once more
Below him at the budding yellow trees
That soon would be a fence of emerald,
Obscuring all beyond except a far
Familiar stillness of eternal hills.
"If we are to believe we have a river,
We must apply the cruel axe, I fancy.
Rivers and trees are an old harmony,
And we, who are not old, may quite as well
Enjoy as lose it."

[32]

                    Gabrielle smiled at him
Impassively. "And we may quite as well
Enjoy as lose each other, I dare say,
And with each other lose all our bad acting.
How in the world should we go on without it?
This morning, before breakfast, you did well—
So very well, to say the truth about it,
That I had anguish to keep up with you;
And I did hardly that, though I did something.
We know each other just enough, my dear,
To be a little sorry for ourselves,
And so a little careful. Get an axe,
And let the river and the world look in
Upon us and our joy. I'll sit and watch
The deed, imagining that you are Gladstone."

He shook his head and smiled, as if the smile
Hurt him: "I cannot wonder, or not fairly,
At anything you say, though I may ask
Whether or not through all that time behind me
When I was lost in hell, you were like this.
If so you were, praise God I never knew it.
You tell me I was acting when a mirror

Made sure this morning I was here again,
And here alive?   I should not name it so.
And were it even so—and you know better—
Is there not hid somewhere, for some of us
To find, a mystery that we may name
The joy of being?   You have heard of it."

"Yes, I have read about it in a book;
And once I knew it.   That was long ago.
Assuming, then, your face was not a fiction,
And I'm aware enough that it was not,
How much of *me* was there in all that rapture?"

"You might have seen by looking in my eyes,
But your eyes only laughed and looked away
Whenever they met mine.   Are mine so dimmed
That they may see in yours no more concern
For my escape than a laugh says they do?
There are more comical occurrences
Than coming out of death to life again.
I know the old house of our other love
Is only a poor ruin falling now
To dust, which if we stir it only chokes us.

My way would be to wreck the remnant of it,
And let the fire of our intelligence
Burn down to honest earth the residue.
Then over the few ashes we may find,
My way would be to let new vision build
With new love a new house.   Am I a fool,
Saying this, or am I no more than peculiar?"

He waited, armored against all surprise
When only a thin smile was her first answer.
"You are an angel, and, for all I know,
A carpenter—but how are you to build
This house, and out of what?   New love?   New vision?
Where do we buy these things?   I'm not assured
That you will build this house."

                              "Never alone,
God knows.   Yet if you cared enough to try,
There might be still an unforeseen adventure
Awaiting you and your indifference.
With all so new around you, possibly
You might be sorry when your memory told you,

If so it ever should, why there are now
No more of us than you and I together."

"And have you not the Raven? Without him,
What else might you not be without this morning?
And what would you be doing now all alone—
With only me? And what would you be seeing?
I'm sure that you would not be standing here,
Or seeing here such a pretty fire of ruins.
I told you all about the skeletons
That we should be by this time without him.
Would any children take the place of him?
Would you exchange for them the miracle
Of your release, rebirth, or what-you-call-it?
I'm almost wholly certain you would not.
Let me be stricken only with a face
A little harder for your contemplation,
And I'll see new love running like a hero
Out of a haunted tomb."

                              He bit his lips
Indignantly and slowly walked away—
Into the hall and back again: "If this

That you are saying had yourself in it,
If I had never known you and your eyes
Without your mask, I might assuredly
Believe, and with a reason, that somewhere
Among your forbears in forgotten ages
There was a colder fish than any swimming
Today in any ocean."

                    "And if you,"
She said, "should go on so ferociously,
I might believe, and with a reason also,
That you have in you more of your grandfather
Than you or I supposed. If you pursue
These revelations of my lineage,
Your words will haunt me like that creature's face,
And I'll be surely scared." She glanced at him
With a quick flash of insecurity,
And added, "I am half afraid already;
Not of your friend, or of your grandfather,
But of this queer new house that you are building
Of timber out of trees that never grew.
For even a phantom house, if made unwisely,
May fall down on us and hurt horribly.

I know enough of houses to say that,
For I have built them."

　　　　　　　"You have never built
The house that I see rising in the light
Around me now," he said, and fixed his words
With a taut smile of courage.

　　　　　　　"Nor have you,"
She told him slowly, gazing at the river.
"If you attempt it, you are to find out,
I fear, that you are not the carpenter
That your spring fiction makes of you this morning.
I know that in your eyes I'm not abhorrent,
As you know that in mine you are no more so;
I know the world has yet for us an envy,
Observing us in our felicity,
As I know the world's envy cannot last.
If you believe that I should go away,
No clubs or whips or tears or indirections
Will be required of your sincerity,
And I shall ask of you no gold.　Forgive me!"

His only answer was a broken smile,
Until at last, after a shrug, he spoke:
"I'll go so far this time as to forgive you,
Although for no deserving qualities
Of afterthought, my dear, in your defection.
I think we see a little better now
The work of those black years when I was blind.
You suffered, and were dismally alone,
But why, for God's sake, have it out of me
In your sad acrobatics of new language.
If there's to be the ceremonial
Of your forgiving of each empty day
That I have made for you unwillingly,
Your task is hard; and even when you are old,
And I am in my grave, your withered zeal
Will have its occupation to the end.
If we are to do nothing but remember,
I'd say with you that you had better go,
And I go after you, and after us
The world—or all that most of it remembers."

"You mentioned, I believe," she said, amused
Indifferently, "a tongue that you defined

[39]

As my new language, and there you surprised me;
For mine is older than the Jebusites,
While yours came yesterday. You understand it—
You and your new-born wisdom, but I can't;
And there's where our disaster, like a rat,
Lives hidden in our walls. In your new house
There would be certainly another like him.
You know it, yet you cannot make yourself
Believe your knowledge; and I'm only asking,
In my poor only way, if this be wisdom.
If your illumination will be honest,
You'll see in this the shadow of a color
Of that which is not altogether true.
A sudden ugliness on me, my dear,
Would make it all so comprehensible!"

Bartholow threw his hands up hopelessly:
"What is it? Would you have me on my knees?
Or why do you insist on this invention?"

"By no means. You would not believe yourself
More there than on your feet. Nor should I like
Your unfamiliar picture of submission:

The whip-hand, though it flourish over us
Only a lash of fancy, has effect.
I see the Raven coming up the hill."

They scanned each other's eyes, but hers were fixed
Not long on his before they flinched again
And looked away from him.   He gazed at her
As at a stranger in a sanctuary,
Then past her at the trees along the river
Until her silence told him she was moving.
"I understand," he said; and his words followed
Her slow unguided steps.   "I understand;
I am not worthy of your mysteries."

III

BARRING an amateur alacrity
   In woodmanship, Bartholow found himself
Content with earthy toil well done by those
Who found in him an easy overseer,
Though not an eyeless one. "You manage others
More than yourself," Penn-Raven told him once,
While yet the demons held him; "for those devils
Had coiled a snare for you so cunningly
That long before your knowledge they had caught you;
And after that their evil diligence
Was only by degrees to weave around
Your being, with invisible tight threads
A thing that, were it not so mortal close,
Would be more like a shroud than you imagine."
But now the shroud, or name it as he would,
Was gone; and in the freedom of his arms
He felt the call of action. "Get your axe,"

His wife had said, and laughed.   He thought of that;
Yet in it there was nothing humorous
While he was there alone; nor, when Penn-Raven,
Approaching, was apprised of her advice,
Was there in his abetting indolence
An overplus of wholesome comedy.
All comedy had faded for the nonce;
And even as nature mostly rubbed along
Without it, so might he, or for a morning.
"There are more axes in the world than one,"
He told his guest; "and there are several trees."

Penn-Raven shook his head and found a chair.
"My vision of your toiling in the distance
Will do for one of you and me together,"
He said.   "The sound of your vicarious axe
Will do the rest.   I shall be happy here,
Knowing that you are strong and on your feet,
And therefore, in a measure, like Antæus,
Who, I believe, was not above the soil
In his activities.   Because your soul
Has found itself and is at last alive,
Never believe that you have not a body.

Lose that, and off your soul will go again
Into the dungeon where it was I found you,
And you will go there with it. Get your axe;
And I'll sit here, saying that you are Gladstone."

Bartholow sighed and answered wearily,
"I wonder if you know how many flies
Are on the roof; or maybe you don't hear them.
If not, why am I hearing the same name
Twice in a morning in the same connection?"

"Coincidence, my friend; coincidence—
And fame. If you are truly celebrated,
Your great toe is immortal. Get your axe,
And let us have a more sufficient view
Of your inspiring river. I like rivers
Better than oceans, for we see both sides.
An ocean is for ever asking questions
And writing them aloud along the shore.
Rivers are not monotonous."

                        "They may be—
Sometimes," Bartholow answered. "If you see

Too far down into them, they may be worse.
I have seen more in this one, in time past,
Than I wish ever to see out of it,
While time endures. But that's all over now."
He smiled, and with an effort brought a laugh
Up from somewhere within him, while Penn-Raven,
Like a ripe artist sure of his achievement,
Surveyed his living work affectionately,
And with a questioning of whether man
Or God were to be garlanded.

Far down
Below him he heard soon, luxuriously
Approving it, the sound of Bartholow's
Industrious axe—with intermittent gaps
Of silence, after which no clearing crash
Had altered yet the scene. A woman's face
Without the falling down of any tree
Before she came, was adequate for that.
He rose, and having found another chair
For Gabrielle, who sat with folded hands
And listened like one hearing something else
Than axes, "He's alive again," he said;

[45]

"Or we should hear no music of that nature
Now on the morning air."

                    She closed her eyes,
As if in his originality
All thought had foundered, and then opened them
As with an interest.   "He will cut one down,"
She told him, in an odd domestic way
That he found somehow more disquieting
In her than scorn or satire would have been.
"He'll cut one down," she said again, more slowly,
"And then come up for Cyrus.   I can see him
As well as if I saw him.   His arms ache,
And he's already wishing that he hadn't."

"I doubt if you need worry or be sorry
For any long time over that," he said,
Smiling away a frown whereat she laughed
As she had laughed before at Bartholow.
"A little seasoning will do his arms
And all the rest of him a year of good
Without it; for he's not long out of prison,
As he would say; and even a prison like his,

Without a purpose or alternative,
Is not the place where a sick soul, alone,
Makes even a giant stronger than he was
Before the door closed on him in the dark.
And he, be it said for his felicity
And his longevity, was not a giant,
Even before there was a darkness for him.
I said 'alone,' because you said it first,
When you saw no more reason to be silent
Where silence would have been, or so it was
You made me to believe, as false to fate,
If that were possible, as to yourself.
Otherwise there had been two silences
About the place—or three, remembering yours."

He saw the gradual tension of her lips
Relaxing, as if words they first had held
Imprisoned were no longer fighting her:
"Mine was a silence, then, to be remembered?
Thank you for that. Thank you for telling me,
Although you were so near forgetting it,
That I may have a silence too that counts.
God knows how drearily I counted it,

If you do not—you men. When I was little,
I'm told that I would howl astonishingly
When there was nothing but myself and silence
To entertain me; and as I stare back
Into some nearer years that now, thank heaven—
And you—are ended, I am ready enough
To say I may have been, when I was forming,
Quite as inadequate for my destiny
As many, I fear, have pardonably inferred
Since then. If you had come a season later
I shiver to think what noises out of me
There might have been, even here—though I'm a child
No longer. It was coming to be creepy,
With only my remembrance of a man
I married once, before he lost himself,
Moving about the house for company—
Nor often moving. He would sit for hours
Trying to make believe that he was reading,
While all he read, as he has told me since,
Was in a language where the words were gone
Like stars under a cloud. Sometimes he feared
The cloud would melt and he should see the words.
To see them, or to fear them without seeing,

Was equally to be alone in hell,
He said,—to be alone without the pleasure
Of even the damned as a companionship;
Though all the time, and once I told him so,
He had forgotten me; for I was there.
There were three years of that, and then . . ."

                              "Well, what?"
Penn-Raven said. "Or was your pause to mean
That I shall tell you? How am I to know?
Once I believed I knew—not long ago
In time, but longer in eternity,
Which is not time. I wonder if you know
Just where the difference is between the two,
Or if there be one—or one more abysmal
Than say between a long year and a short one,
A false one and a real one? Once I believed
I knew more than I know—or so it seems.
If you are still alone, where shall I say
That I am? Will you look at me and answer?
I am not asking much in saying that,
For I am asking only everything—
Which in our coin of words may more than often

Weigh less than little. If you made me rich
With a false gold that one may count as real
Only in dreams, you cannot have it back,
For now it is all gone. There's no need now
Even to look for it. Will you look at me?"

"Assuredly," she said, obeying him
With languid and reluctant eyes half shut
Against the fire in his. "Is that enough?"

"No," he said slowly, as her flinching gaze
Looked off uneasily into the distance;
"No, not if you are asking for the truth;
And even if you do ask it, who am I
That I should venture now to say for you
A thing that you know best, or should know best,
Without a man's tuition or assistance?
I think of only one thing I may say,
And one that will add little to your store,
Where you fling everything indifferently
Into the dark and leave it unappraised.
You see there's hanging somewhere between heaven
And earth, where heaven is earth and earth is heaven,

A region where no argument avails.
We stay, or go. I do not say it matters—
When we are dead."

                    "You've said we never die,"
She answered,—"and almost as if you knew it;
But there I've always had my little doubt.
You may for every other mortal question
Be the one man alive with the last answer,
Yet I am no more sad than I am happy
For cleaving to at least one ignorance
Where even the smallest of us are as great
As are the giants. There's one democracy
Where I'm at home to all; and there's no other."

"My theme was farther from democracy
Than your illusions are from your evasions."
There was a darker fire now in his eyes
Than hers had fire to meet; and though she smiled,
She felt the searing of his inquisition
Like white iron on her soul. "All I may say
Might well be wished unsaid, or better so.
Say we are whirling amid spheres of reason,

[51]

Our floating out of one into another
May prove a sorry voyage if we forego
The plain way to the shore of our departure;
Say we are less than our pursuing forces,
We may be stricken early in our flight,
And after an obscure awakening
May find ourselves elsewhere no further on
In our escape from our discrepancies
Than here among them; and we may not all,
Even there, be sure we see how vain it was
To cloud them with illusions and evasions
Like yours. And if there burrow among others
Many who see no more than you are seeing
In your disheartened hunger for escape,
I might say there was vision in their blindness—
If I saw more than truth."

                    "What more is there
Than truth for you to see," said Gabrielle,
Her lips grown tight again, "in all your spheres?
If truth be all it is that we are after,
What more is there before us when we have it?
I'm not so much a tenant of the spheres

As you are—and I don't much like 'escape';
I'd hardly say it was the only word,
Considering all there are, for you to fling
So freely at me—now. There may be others
More to the purpose. I shall not know men,
Though I live on till all humanity
Be dry bones at my feet, and the world frozen."

The bitterness of his anticipation
Was in her speech, and it remained alive,
Surviving utterance in her brittle smile;
And it was of a savor to endure
As long with him as were the strokes he heard
Of an unconscious and relentless axe,
Below him and unseen. He counted them
As if he were the tree on which they fell,
Feeling them as apparently the tree did;
Though in their stubborn echo there was yet,
For him who listened where his injured wonder
Saw fronting him the grave of more than life,
A thrill wherein he shared ingenuously
The salvage of another's resurrection.

IV

EARLY one silent evening in July,
Faintly aware of roses and syringas,
And of a steely glimpse of quiet water
Through boding trees below him in the light
Of a huge moon above the distant hills,
Penn-Raven paced alone over the flags
That were a floor outside the ivied house
Where he had been too long—unwillingly
At first, as he believed, and latterly
Without the will to go. "All this will end,"
He thought, in the old way of all who think
Too little and too late; "and when all this
Is ended, the same moon will shine again
As it shines now, and over the same river.
The river and the moonlight and the trees,
When I am gone, will be as when I came—
The same, all but the trees. A few of them,

And eminently one, will not be here."
A fragile smile upon a solid face
Told of a sharp remembrance.

                              Bartholow,
Coming unheard out of a silent house,
And all unconscious then of one so near him,
Gazed over the calm shine of broken water
And upward at the sky over the hill,
And at the moon. "God!" he said, half aloud;
"God, what it is to be alive again!
I hope there is at least one other man
Somewhere on earth who knows."

                              The fragile smile,
Unseen behind him, suddenly was a laugh—
Though not, if Bartholow had measured it,
Quite that of an imaginary colleague
Sharing a new born rapture like his own
Of living in a new world after dying
In one that was no more. "Let both of us
Hope there is one at least," Penn-Raven said,
Out of a shadow; "and there may be two.

[55]

Somewhere among the world's invisible millions
There may be two—or three.   And if I may,
I'll ask if your eccentric preparation
For gliding off alone into the silence—
First having praised the Lord, and properly—
Has any crude significance.   Your stick
Would hardly crush an enemy's cranium,
You are no virtuoso in your fists,
And I can see no violence in your eyes,—
For which, may peace attend you."

                       "I am going,"
Bartholow said, "for the new joy of moving.
It was a nine days' wonder for nine days,
And after ninety is a wonder still.
Don't ask, I pray, if I'm in any doubt
Of whence it came, or if I'm small enough
To figure in a dream of idiocy
That if I should assign to you for ever
All that I have, or may have, to call mine,
I should pay half of one forlorn per cent
Of all I owe to you.   Remember that;
And when I walk away from you alone,

Leaving you here behind me uninvited,
Say 'There goes one so glad to be himself
That he deserts the friend who made him so.'
And that will tell you all; or if not all,
More than enough. There comes along an hour
When we find even our saviours in the way,
And we are best alone. My darkest urging
Tonight is for a walk along the river.
We see it better than once on a time,"

"We do," Penn-Raven answered absently;
And added instantly, "We do, indeed.
It was a memorable tree, my lord,
That you brought down for us that sunny morning;
And you, craving your grace, were some time at it.
I'll hardly see the falling of one like it
Before I'm off again for other regions.
God knows you've paid in hospitality
Your fee a thousand told, and then a thousand—
If you persuade your eccentricity
Still to believe there ever was a fee.
Transform your ledger, leaving your red lines
And digits on my side; for I'm in debt

[57]

Immeasurably to you; and have been so
For gain past all our counting. Where's the use
Of counting when you know that I shall pay
In gold about the time I pay in blood?
My one defense of my persistence here
Is in yourselves and your unleavable
Domain—and, since your triumph, in your river.
It was a tree indeed that you brought down.
When I'm away, I shall still hear that axe."

"No, no,—some other evening, when it rains,"
Bartholow answered, lightly, "we'll attend
To these obscure details of your departure;
By which I mean that I'll do anything
But urge a man to stay. If you agree,
We'll wait until it rains."

                              "I may do that,"
Penn-Raven said. "I may, or I may not;
For even a friend may ride his best friend's patience
Until it founders like a worn out horse.
With your connivance I'll not wait for that.
By which I mean, you are a patient host;
Though ever since the downfall of that tree,

[58]

There's been a burden on you. I have seen it,
And I have borne it with you, saying nothing.
There may or may be not for me a moment
When I shall ask you sometime to believe
Tradition less than life, and shipwreck worse
Than anchorage in time—though pride may twitch
A while at your composure. If I'm wrong,
And two to one I am, being no prophet
Of more than your continued usefulness,
You may forgive an honest awkwardness,
Praising your fate that I'm not here much longer
To brush your kingly velvet the wrong way,
Having done something once to make it smoother.
Meanwhile, the event of my still being here
When you return from your noctambulism
Is clamped with all the probabilities.
My eyes are always on the probable.
Poor in all else, I'm rich in my conceit
Of seeing that if I say too much at once
Your prayer will be for rain before tomorrow."

Bartholow, startled into indecision,
Answered him with a lightness like to that

Of a weight raised with an unwonted ease:
"To say that I've no glimpse of what you see
Would be a waste of blindness, and a lie;
Yet I conceive you wrong. When I come back,
If in the mood I will say more of this;
And if not now, surely that rainy night
I mentioned, soon or later, will occur,
When I may have to hold you here to listen,
If only for an evening—which, I trust,
Will not come on too soon; for when you go,
You will be taking more away with you
Than I may look to find again elsewhere,
Though I should wander always after it.
Remember that; and let your memory
Be sure you keep it warm till I return.
Where should I be by now if a friend's fancy
Had never sent you here as a last hope
That you might cure the lame and make him walk?
Well, he can walk. Observe him." Saying that,
He stepped along the gravel jauntily,
Leaving a friend for whom at least the sky
Was all a confirmation of no rain.

"In what the devil does he 'conceive' me wrong?"
Penn-Raven thought. "And in what am I right,
If not in saving while it may be saved
All there is left, if there be anything left,
For him? I'm witness to futilities,
And I believe he knows it, that may wreck him
Before he sees that he is on the rocks
That he'll not say are waiting where a dark
And silent water that lies over them
Inveigles him along to immolation
I cannot see before him with his eyes,
And would not if I could—come what may come."

He sat for a time watching, lazily,
The moonshine on the water through the trees,
Wondering when he might again, if ever,
Revisit, save in a wan memory,
This glimmering scene of all that he had lost
Before he knew that he had never found it.
It was an easy fancy to be seeing
Himself there as a ghost alone outside
A lighted ruin where he knew there lived
Another ghost, and one that had of late

Said little for his ears.   After a time,
Assured and reassured that he had felt
The dying of his last uncertainties,
An anguish born of battling recollections,
And of an evening-hidden host of odors
Thrown on him by leaf-shielded moon-black blossoms,
Choked him and held him for as long as death.
Then he went calmly into his friend's house
And laid his thick lips closely upon those
Of his friend's wife, who, toiling with a book,
Was reading wearily of deeds remote
From all abrupt and amorous interventions.
Before she noticed him or said a word,
She pushed away his head, and with a cry
Stifled insensibly into a gasp
Of anger mixed with a remembered fear,
She stared away from him and at a window—
Where there was nothing more that was in sight
Than a few clumsy moths indignantly
Refusing to be free.

                    "Were you afraid?"
He said.   And from his question Gabrielle

Could isolate combined regret, reproach,
Pride, misery and farewell. "Were you afraid—
Afraid of me? Or was it mostly anger?
I should have said it was a little late
To be afraid, though only the Lord knows
What women are afraid of, or what not.
Of course I beg your pardon, for I feared
That if I waited for it I should lose it."

She sat with her eyes fixed upon the window,
But not as if she saw it any longer;
And when she turned them finally on him
He chose to see more fear than anger in them.
"I'll tell you one thing women are afraid of,"
She said. "They are afraid of being seen
In arms of other men than have a right
To hold them. If I'm rather vague about it,
Or if in your opinion I'm eccentric,
Forgive me. Yes, I was a moment frightened."

"Not of those foolish moths outside the screen,
I hope. Having outworn their metaphors,
Now they are wearing out their silly wings.
They are the same as always, and no wiser."

"I never told you, but a week ago
You heard him, and you must remember him.
I felt the presence of eyes looking at us
Through the same window, but you let me go
Before I was afraid, and that was all—
Till I heard some one shuffling at the door.
It was that awful beast who brought the fish,
And I stood facing him. I saw his eyes
That night, and I have seen them ever since.
He brought a book, and said his wretched name
Was Umfraville; and then he went away.
I fancy we have had him here before
Of evenings—though by chance, or providence,
I have not had to see him. Now there's one
Dark mystery the less in a dark world—
If you remember such a thing as breakfast,
And my not eating it."

                        "I do," he said.
"I do; but there are memories more intense,
As there are disillusions more enduring,
And revelations that are more destroying,
Than all your portraitures and premonitions

Of this ill-favored bookworm may inflict
On me and my departure. When I go,
I shall have brought one man to life again,
And in so doing shall have lost all else
Than life, and more than life. You question that,
And with a reasoning unimpeachable;
For none may lose what he has not to lose,
Or find again what never has been his.
I say this only for the barren gain
Of saying it; though as you see me now,
Knowing that I had better never more
Be near you, nor say more to you hereafter,
Or you to me, my dream denies my knowledge."

Slowly she clutched and held with angry fingers
The book that she was reading when he came,
And looked away until in her cold eyes,
Now meeting his again, he felt a gleam
Of bitter patience and of resignation.
"If I have more to give than I have given,"
She said, glancing away from him a little,
"Many would say to you it is my life.
And if I cannot say so, and say truly,

[65]

You may as well know why—though I've a guess
That somewhere in your tragic suavity
I may have missed a murmur on your part,
Or lost a warning, that I may as well
Say nothing. Are you sure that you know why?"

"I am not sure that I know anything,"
Penn-Raven said, "except that I was blind;
And that my one illusion of defence
Was gone before my plunging trust in it
Would let me see that I was blind. Belief
Is easy where the wish is to believe,
Or so it has been said,—and I believed.
If in your reason for not saying something
You see an end that's worth a journey there,
Go on; and as I may, I'll follow you.
I see but one end, and I don't see that."

"Whatever the worth, or lack of it, be now,"
She said, with a sharp languor that had claws,
"You may as well sit down. If you stand up,
You may be seen by someone else outside.
If that unhappy monster comes again

He'll wonder what you mean by glowering at me
As if I were a serpent in a garden.
That was a flecting pleasantry of mine
At which you might have smiled. My reason, then,
For saying that my life is not the most
That I have not yet given to you, is this—
And it is only this: My life is less
To me tonight than I may give a stranger
Out of my purse, to keep him warm and fed
Till he forgets me. If my life would save him,
And make him happy till he died in peace,
I'm not so sure tonight he mightn't have it,
If he could have it quickly. You may say,
And safely, that I'm shooting a new arrow
At a new target without hitting it—
If so you like,—yet I've a childish wish
That you remember me when you are gone
As one who at a pinch remembered others,
And did a little good. Your tragedies,
Your revelations and your disillusions,
Are blows that with a struggle I dare say
One might survive. Are you the only one
Who has had revelations, disillusions,

Tragedies? When you came you found me sick
To desperation with all three. The rest
I take upon myself. Call me all names
There are that are not complimentary,
But never tell me that I cast on you
The burden or the blame. It was all one—
Or so I thought it was—and I was here,
Prowling about eternally alone,
And always in the dark. It was all dark
Until you came from nowhere with a lamp;
And if I read more by the light of it
Than once I fancied I should ever read,
You do not hear me saying I was blind.
I am no blinder now than I was then;
And I've a notion, when the worst is over,
You'll find your way along with no great anguish.
Men have incurred more woe for sterner trials
Than you for yours, and they have suffered less."

He saw that while she spoke her lips were shaking,
And in the poise of her dry monotone
He felt a quiver of weak scorn that failed;
And while he studied her unhappy eyes,

[68]

In which a mist was imminent, he smiled,
Impassively, as a physician might
At a brave invalid's improvisations,
And shook his head: "Your life is less, you say,
To you than a vague benefit bestowed
On those who for your purpose, one infers,
Might throw the needless baggage of their names
Into the rivers of annihilation—
As you, in turn, might throw into your river
As many nameless pebbles. And the rest
You take upon yourself, indifferently.
What if it happens you have not so much
As fate has, in the way of a last word,
To say of what it is that you may take
So lightly, and upon yourself alone?
There are some burdens that are borne alone,
And there are some that settle heavily,
Grinding as hard, and harder, upon those
Who mimic the oblivious and immune.
We are all players to our necessities,
But here tonight there is no need of playing;
And when I go away from here tomorrow,
Out of your sight and back again to nowhere,

Leaving you free to count your store again,
You may discover there is more in you
Left yet for living than you say there is."

"You qualify the picture with a tinge
Of your own color, as you always do,
And always did," she said, evading him.
"Women are more proficient, we are told,
In these accomplishments than men.   No matter;
I drew at least an outline.   If you fail
To like it, or to see the merit of it,
I'm without art and without interest
Enough to make another for you now."

He shook his head again at her, and sighed.
"You'll go no farther on the wings of that
Than a few dusty flutterings may take you
Along the ground.   And if I say just why,
Candor may soon be driving both of us
Into a rough and unfamiliar region,
So near that you may think it more remote
From where you are than childhood or the grave.
When there, I'll only hope a glimpse of truth

[70]

May not surprise you, or dishearten you
Beyond endurance. When you said before
That all was dark when I came here to you,
You saw beyond the frontier, but not far;
And you were not there long enough to say
That when I came there were two darknesses,
And one the darker for the light you made.
At first you found only a stranger here;
And on approaching and observing him
As well as an enforced and endless groping
After the shine of almost any light
But yours would let you think that you had seen him,
You thought him an obscure adventurer,
No doubt,—if not a charlatan, or worse—
Until you knew that he was innocent
Of all contrivance or black stratagem,
Which would have been concealed about as well
From you as would your river from the moon;
And then you knew, as you must know tonight,
That he had found in you all he had sought,
Past hope of any finding. All was wreck
Around you; and he saw no other light,
In or about the place, than your pale fire,

Fading and all but lost.   And then it was
He found in him that had you as a wife
One he could see that was for you no longer
More than another stranger in a cave—
Indifferent there to you and to your guidance,
If that would be its name.   So many changes
Have altered you since then, that all I know
For certain is that if you know yourself,
You know too much for your tranquillity."

"If I am such a cold chameleon
As that," she said, hiding a furtive yawn,
"Your warmth—or I've a notion so—is wasted.
You cannot make a lizard any warmer
By catching it and saying it's a lizard.
Moreover, I'm an atom less acquainted
Than you appear to be with all these changes.
I wonder if by some capricious chance
They may be rather yours than mine—these changes;
For surely you are not as you were then,
More than the Roman Bartholow I married
Is now as he was when you came to him.
You made him over, but I'm asking yet

How such an awkward mingling of the soul
And body as there is in your medicine
Had virtue to restore him.   All the same,
I would not have you think me credulous,
Incurably, for I know as well as you
That his illumination cannot last.
I know it, for I know it never does."

Before she finished there was in his eyes
The gloomy coming of a stormy scowl,
Where now the pride of a sure faith impeached
Told of a disillusion more profound,
At first, than one of love that was unshared—
And lately, with a false and frozen lightness,
Unsought and unacknowledged.   "If you care,"
He said, distinctly, moistening his thick lips,
"Enough about yourself to see tonight
The face of someone in your looking-glass
That you have seen there frequently before,
You may as well begin your banishing
At once of these inept irrelevancies.
If science tells you it was not the soul
That ailed him when I came, why not believe it?

And why, seeing him here alive again
Do you insist that he shall not be here?
These demons of insistence, if encouraged,
May serve you well; for you are not yet old.
Time is alive with opportunities,
And you are here to seize them, if you will."

"Do you mean anything when you say that,"
She asked, "or are you only saying it?"
Her lips were shaking and her cheeks were pale,
And in her eyes there was an anger flashing,
At which he only smiled and shook his head
Once more without an answer. "Are you laughing,"
She said,—"or what, for God's sake, are you doing?
Is this the converse of a woman scorned,
Or are you saying that if I insist,
On heaven knows what, I shall be killing someone?
I may, if I'm annoyed, begin with you—
Though doubtless I shall not. You wouldn't feel it."

He drew his lips in tightly, while his eyes
Revealed again to Gabrielle's cold chagrin
Their calm primeval sheen of innocence

That always had bewildered and accused her.
"Nothing on earth, my child," he said, serenely;
"Nothing, unless to mention generally
That we are all at work on one another
Not knowing how or when, nor, as a rule,
Much caring. If you find you do not care,
You may as well, or better, not be working;
But while you are alive you might regard
A good man's resurrection as no loss
To those who need him in a world where few
Are like him in his coming usefulness.
Whether you do or not, expel forever
All unavailing thought of prodigies
Or miracles I may have exercised.
There is a field for them, or their appearance,
Though I have never gleaned or wandered in it;
There's also an unfailing fountain head
Of power and peace; and if but once we prove
The benefit of its immortal taste,
Our living thirst will have a living drink—
Dilute it or offend it as we may
With trashy draughts of easy consequence,
Mingled with reason."

Gabrielle flung herself
Forward a little, and with cynic triumph,
And with a grateful venom in her voice,
Struck at him like a snake: "Like me, for instance—
Mingled with reason. We'll remember that,
Always. If we forget and leave that out,
The fires of heaven will make an end of us,
And on the instant. What you really mean
Is not that we may fool ourselves for ever,
But rather, 'there's a way that seemeth right,
But the end whereof are the ways of death.' I fancy
The men who made the Proverbs knew as much
About this mingling of our drink as you do.
If I see disapproval in your eyes,
Why do you spare my feelings with a club
When you could hurt me less with a sharp knife?
And if there's anything you've not yet said
For my well-being and advantage, say it;
Only, be sure you mingle it with reason."

"If you compound these incongruities
For your amusement," he said, acridly,
"I cannot answer for your joy of them.

You will remember them when I am gone,
Tomorrow, and will not be glad for them;
And you will see, tomorrow or sometime,
How far the reckless whims of weariness
Are from a love that you have never known,
And have not yet in you the power to know.
Once in a life, they tell us, and once only,
So great a thing as a great love may come—
To crown us, or to mark us with a scar
No craft or custom shall obliterate;
All which may well be true, or partly true,
Or not be true. For you it doesn't matter,
So long as you're at ease with circumstance
And have your eminence of admiration.
Now you are not at ease with anything,
And are as far into the dark again
As when the stranger came. Had he been wiser,
Your beauty and your nearness and your burden
Might not have overwhelmed his loyalty,
Or, for a time, blotted out everything
There was for him but you—and was not you;
Though he believed it was until one day
The fire that he had let you build for him

Upon his altar suddenly went out,
And there was in his temple only smoke
And darkness. It was then for the first time
That he heard your ghost laughing in the darkness,
As he should always have been hearing it—
And would, had he been wiser. You were dead
Before he came, and that's the way it was
That he could hear your ghost. Your sacrifice,
Given as he sees now that it was given,
Is his to pay, not yours. If you have eyes,
You see what he has paid—or he pays twice
In your not seeing. You knew that in his love
You had, whether or not you cared for knowing,
More than a few in any thousand men
May lay upon the altar of one woman;
And, haunting an old ruin as you were then,
You reasoned that another ruin or two
Would not much matter, and in any event
Would be a change. And that was your grand passion."

Gabrielle, staring at him in slow anger,
Saw in his eyes a gleam of mystic hardness;
And then she saw the book that she was holding.

"You make an awful noise over the dead,
At any rate," she said, and said it sharply.
"If I'm to listen to much more of it,
I'll soon be tearing leaves out of this book
And eating them. Is this what we shall hear
In our emancipation from now on?
You've given the pendulum a swing that's fit
To break the wheels; and you have struck me with it.
Forgive me if I seem a little stunned,
Or if my words go wrong, or I say less
Than I might say. If life were more to me,
I might say more of an immortal passion
That only one pure mortal in a million,
Or so I understand, may give a woman—
While she gives nothing. There's a rat somewhere
In your most holy temple. I can hear him."

A sudden fear that anger had released
Within her was now fighting with her heart,
And there was nothing in the room around her
That she had ever seen as now she saw it.
Over the floor before her she could fancy
A chair and a man in it coming nearer,

While in the molten wonder of his eyes,
That were no fancy, she could only watch
The burning of a sad fanatic fire
That she had never seen in them before,
And one she knew that she was not to see
In a man's eyes again. She saw it burning
Until she saw no more; and while he spoke,
Although her eyes were covered with her fingers,
She felt the fire in his, and saw it burning.

"If you have heard what you have heard," he said,
"For what it was I told you, I may toss
The tinsel of your insincerity
Where soon the dust of time will cover it;
But if you heard no more than your perverse
Evasions of it willed that you should hear,
Your life may well be less to you indeed
Than one or other of those easy trifles
That you may fling to those you call your poor.
Who are the rich to you, and who the poor?
You have brought one man nearer to the shreds
Of living death than you may bring another,
And there is yet yourself. You are still here,

And if your dream is to live on with him,
No house that you and he may build together
Will stand long on a lie; and if you choose
To tell him all, there will not be a house
For you to build. Let the worst be the worst—
Though I hope not—well, then, it matters not,
Or not this time. You are yourself—no other—
And we that are ourselves are all or nothing;
And if life, as I view it, has a reason,
Death is among the least of little things.
If there's within you, and I hope there is,
A power to rend the shell you cannot see
That in your loneliness has grown around you,
And yet may crush you, make of it all you may.
For, if there be within you no such power,
If there be only what you say there is,
You are too beautiful to be alive."

V

WHEN he had watched her there for a time longer
    With the same eyes, he left her where she was
And vanished heavily. She could see him going,
Although she saw him not; and she could see
His eyes, although they were no longer there
For her to see. To know that she was burned,
There was no need to touch the fire again
That burned her; and she knew there was no cure
In asking why. "Why, then," she asked herself,
"Did I sit here before him for so long,
Like a vain martyr willing to be tortured?"
And that was her one question till another
Came slowly out of silence, like a face
Out of a shadow, coming cruelly
And bringing with it only the same answer.
If there was any other to be found,
It was her task, and hers alone, to find it.

There might be one, if she looked hard enough
Into herself to see; for it was there,
And only there, she knew, that she might read it—
If there it was. Others had found elsewhere
Their answer, but their fortune was not hers;
For she had not their vision for the dark,
And had not their invisible clue to follow.

She gazed about the room with frightened eyes,
In a child's way, as if in a child's hope
That what she sought might yet be found where search
Repeated yielded nothing but the same
Dark empty places. Weary at last of that,
Her questioning deserted the dim walls
And corners, and the silence of the floor,
For the cold shining surface of a table,
Whereon were scattered things of common use,
That lay as they had lain there before clouds
Had wrapt her days with night and stifled them
Till day was night within her and around her.
They had outlived it all, and were the same
As they had been when all was unrevealed
That was to come before it was revealed,

And as they would be still, there or somewhere,
When Bartholow and Gabrielle were names
That none remembered. What was it all for,
Unless, indeed, as her inquisitor
Had said before he vanished,—for a reason?
If he said right, why were so few to know
That reason, or to know there was a reason,
Or to believe they knew? To think of him,
And still to see him there as she had seen him
Only an age of minutes past, and still
To endure the nameless calm and virulence
Of his invective, and his blasting eyes,
Renewed in her an undulating rage
That slowly rose until it broke and fell
Vainly upon a wreck that long had been
Adrift and empty, and worth no more wrecking.
Already it had broken many times;
And if again, or many times again,
What of it? There would be no more next time
For it to fall upon than there was now.
The fire that smote so deep had smitten less
Than he supposed, for there was less to smite;
And the waves coming after were no more

Than waves at midnight on an empty ocean.
So—let them come, she thought; and then considered
Bartholow for a while, who had not come.
He had seen much in his illumination—
Failing a better name for the unknown—
That she, having a soul that had no eyes,
If she had any, had not been born to see;
And he had suffered hard. She knew all that,
If she knew nothing else. And if a man
Had suffered much to see, had not a woman
Suffered as much not seeing? Gabrielle,
Recalling how the sunshine wakened her
Upon the morning of her wedding day,
Remembered that she went to sleep again;
And now she wondered, in a misty way,
What might have come to pass if they had given
Themselves back to each other before chains
They might have broken then, or broken since,
Had held them, and so given back all those years
That now could not be given. For they were gone,
Those years with him; and what was coming now?
She did not know. There was a way to know
And one that made her lips quiver again

[85]

Unwillingly, and brought, for the first time,
Tears to her eyes tonight.   Her eyes were hot
With too much gazing into a dark fire
Before its angry devastation came
To waste itself on what was left of her
And leave it scorched; and while her tears ran down
Over her face they were not washing off,
She knew, the scars that were for Bartholow
To see and read—if he still cared enough,
Once having seen them there when he came back,
More than to see them there.   In such a thought
There was a prowling hope that smothered fear,
And there was a quick fear that strangled hope.
But now it was not fear, and was not hope,
That weakly would have stretched the severed ends
Of worldliness together; for the strands
That once were soft were sodden now, and frayed
Beyond all tying.   And if they were tied,
The knot would always be a knot.

                              Once more
Her search went creeping over rugs and walls
And into corners, where, among the shadows,

Nothing that was the shadow of an answer
Was there that she had overlooked. Her eyes,
At last refusing to stare any longer
At always the same vacant shapes and patterns,
Grew blind again with tears of weariness
And weary pain; and she could feel once more
Their flowing fire. If she could be afraid,
Then pity, when Bartholow came back, might wring
From fear somehow an answer; and if then
She told him, out of pity might rise hope,
And out of hope might rise that house of his.
Employing hope, they might begin to build it,
Knowing that it would not last very long,
And yet when it was there, and they were in it,
Would be a sort of house the while it lasted—
Although there were some phantom rats in it
Already, and more coming. "God, what a house
That house will be!" she thought; and though new tears
Were flowing hot out of her eyes again,
She laughed—until her fancy was a mirror
Wherein she recognized herself and hated
All that she saw. She felt her body shaking,
Partly in anger, partly in desolation,

But rather more in a despairing wonder
At all this unintelligible waste
That was her life and should not have been so.
There was no great persuasion she could find
In any text or pretext or lost warning
For all who seize on comfort without love;
There were too many who had seized and held it,
Giving romance no more ascendency
Than honor might allow, and so, in time,
Gone their allotted and unspotted ways
Into their tombs, with no interrogations
After their unoffending epitaphs.
And so she would have gone, had all gone well,
And had the destinies been rational,
Instead of casting her into this pit
Where there was only darkness and a scrap
Of night above that was another darkness.
And so she would have gone, she said again,
Had all gone well. There was no doubt of it,
She said, had all gone well; and said it over,
Until at last those four cold heavy words
Were like the slow, incessant falling down
Of four hot hammers on a brain that ached

Like the bruised body of a beaten child,
Until again a freezing clutch of triumph—
One she had felt a thousand times before
And had as frequently before put off—
Drew her, it seemed, away from under them.
"Well, when he comes, he comes; and after that,
What matters it what comes?" Here was a question,
If there was not another in the world,
That she might answer.

         While she answered it
She heard the crunching of his coming feet
Along the gravel, and then on the stones
She heard them coming; and she heard them now
Inside the silent house. Into the room
They came, and there they waited. "So?" he said;
"So near asleep as that, and all alone?
Where is the Raven?"

         She looked up at his face,
Measuring in her mind a change on hers
That was by now beyond all artifice
To conquer or conceal. Bartholow frowned
On Gabrielle, or so she believed then,

With a confirming flash of accusation
That she had long awaited, and sometimes,
Like one too long condemned without a charge
And then forgotten, more than half wished to see.
But she had never found it until now;
Yet now she found it, and was not yet sure
Where most his wound would be. "The Raven talked
So long," she said, with an unreal precision
That pierced him as he listened, "that I . . ."

                       "Yes?"
Bartholow said, like a machine. "He talked
So long that you . . ."

                "Yes," Gabrielle said slowly;
"He talked so long to me that I dismissed him—
Or let him go. At any rate, he went.
I think he must have gone down by the river,
Unless you met him on the upper road."
The flatness of her saying more like that
Failed in her throat. The rest was a dry cough.

He waited, standing there as he had stood
When he came in, and as he might have stood

Had he been clay upon an armature
Instead of injured flesh and hidden bones.
"I have not seen him on the upper road,
Or any road. What have you two been saying
To make a death's head of you in an hour?
I'm not a man to make wild elephants
Of mice and squirrels, yet if you have leisure,
I'll stay at home a while till I know more.
Since my return back to the world again,
I may have been too much away from here—
Too much in the woods, may be. If I sit down,
The picture of us here alone together
Will be more homelike and more sociable.
It will be like old times."

                    In the same chair,
And with a nonchalance more devastating
After Penn-Raven's tyrannous reproach,
Bartholow, like a new inquisitor,
Had now the other's place. His eyes were bright
With healthy calm, and in them Gabrielle
Saw yet no veiled combustion, or a sign
Of any conflagration that was coming.

Rather in their cool gaze there was a quiet
That was almost content—or might have been,
Could they have been less cool. They were not cold,
But they might soon become so, and so freeze
All her indifference to a slow death,
Leaving the rest of her that was alive
To grope alone for lost obscurities.

"From all this wreckage that he left behind,
One might—without imagining unduly—
Build evidence of a storm," he said at length,
With a selective accent and a poise
Too sure for certainty. "Why should a storm
Be falling on us now, and with a sky
That is all moon and stars and quietness?
I'm sure that no injurious elements
Have been at work outside; yet in this room,
Or rather on your face, there are the marks
Of an uncommon crash. Have you been trying,
By any chance, to build yourself a house
With me away, and after a new plan
That I might not approve? If you do so,
Your private architecture may collapse

[92]

With a worse fall than you foresaw for mine
One rare spring morning. Are you more adept
Than all those ancient forces that are able
To wear down even the strongest of our houses?
Sometimes I'd say it was a miracle
Of God that holds the best of them together
While we, with our peculiar properties,
Not yet appraised, are moving into them.
I wonder why so many of them stand—
Or if they would so long without the props
Of caution that should be invisible.
I wonder why so many of them last—
Or if they do. All this, of course you see,
Is merely my ephemeral speculation.
Only of late have just a few queer flashes
Been sharp enough to make me see them twice—
Once with eyes open, once having closed them tight.
The wise, I fancy, are those who may see nothing
Where there is nothing they would see. Moreover,
I'll owe you an immense apology;
And there's a friend to whom I'll owe another,
Being already his ungracious debtor
For all but everything. If this goes on,

I'll see myself insolvent. And how then
Shall we build houses?"

                "There will be no houses,"
Gabrielle said, scarce knowing when she said it;
"Or none, I mean, that we shall build together.
I might have told you so without your asking;
And once I did so, nearly. But you heard
Only what you would hear. Never mind me,
But build it all alone, or with another
Who will not shake it down over your head,
And over hers. Perhaps if I had known
More than I did, and felt less than I did,
That all was gone and there was nothing coming,
I might have gone before it was all gone.
Before you knew me, it was your conceit
To praise me, saying that I had a mind.
But I should have had more than I did have,
Or less. Either provision might have saved us—
Or me, I mean; for now I can see nothing
Before me, or behind me. It's all gone.
I should have lived in velvet ignorance,
With one to share it and to keep it smooth,

And with a mind that never would have burrowed
As yours did into me to find so little.
I wish you had found less and found it sooner,—
Or more, and only found it. But you failed
In finding either; and that's all of it.
So—why build houses? Other men have built them,
Though often, if not always, I dare say,
In a new place, with new material,—
Ready at hand, or soon to come along
When the old vanishes. *Les morts vont vite*—
Or *Vive la reine;* or one without the other.
The queen may come, or not. How shall I know?"

Bartholow, having driven as he believed
Or fancied he believed, a vicious bolt
At a veiled emblem of uncertainty,
And one that only sorrow and remorse
Together might withdraw, saw Gabrielle
Before him as an unreal mockery
That pride and faith and his infatuation
Had once made real. Now there was nothing real,
Now there was only pride; though for a time
There was a multitude of other names

[95]

That gathered slowly into a dark swarm
Where pride was only one.   He felt their wings
And stings, and while they battened on his pain,
Sat watching Gabrielle until he knew
That she knew more than he of what was gone,
And so had known before there was a friend
To save him and to filch her from his arms.
Whether or not he prized her any more
Than would a Sultan of another language,
And with no mind for blood, prize what a thief
That was a friend had stolen and made his,
The damnable reiterate possessive
Strangled him to an insincerity
That while it numbed him was indifference.
"If she was only that, they're all the same—
Or would be so," he thought; "and all that beauty
Is now no more than a few living cinders,
And ashes that yet live."   He cursed at once
Himself and his avenging fatuousness
For saying a thing like that, even in silence,
And bowed his head.   "Good God!" he said aloud;
And that was all he said for a long time.

Gabrielle heard the moths outside the screen,
Still angry at their freedom, while she faced
A freedom hardly worth another anger
That she felt rising in her at herself,
For being herself. Penn-Raven's anodyne
Of cold assurance after his attack
Had healed her as a dash of icy water
Might heal in her the deep devouring wound
That years had made for minutes to make deeper;
And if in such a wound there was no fear,
More than a weariness of too much pain,
There was no fear left anywhere worth feeling.
He would have told her there was none, she thought
And shivered when she thought of him alive.
Bartholow, knowing only the unknown,
And sharing only the unsharable,
Would have his day; and when his night should come,
He would be free and in the dark again,
Without her for a burden to be lost
In being borne. So now she felt the cold
Of his accusing and inscrutable eyes
With only a blank sorrow for the past,
And with a chilly calm for what was yet

Impending and assured.   There was no hope
Worth delving after in the frozen poise
That held her shifting glance now and again,
But never shifted in its iciness;
And there was neither grief nor wrath betrayed
Where either would have been, by now, to her
An arid and infirm extravagance.

"Why do you tell me now that other men
Have built of their insolvency new houses?
What are all houses that all other men
Have built, or may build, worth to me tonight,
Now that I see no house?   May all go well
With those who are to build and live in them;
But I would rather hear no more of them
While I see mine, or one that in my dream
Would have been mine, ruined and in the dust
Of other dreams.   The time we throw away
On dreams we know that our intelligence
Would laugh at and disown, the devil reckons,
Knowing that we may count so much the less
Against him, having known they were all dreams.
Well, we had better know them and be dead,

Or be alive and leave them dead behind us.
I am not going to die of this, you see,
And you need have no fear that I shall hurt you.
I could not if I would. You are not worth . . .
But no, I was not saying that. I'm sorry.
We'll blot that much away with a black line,
And then forget it. You are too beautiful
To hurt; and you have hurt yourself enough.
You were not made for this; and now you know it—
And why it was that I should know no more
Than to believe in dreams that were for me
Nearer to credence than realities
Were then, or are tonight. You were not made
To throw yourself at the first thing you caught
In your first web. You are not like the spider.
She lets a prey too strong break as he will
Her net and fly away from her again.
You should have done so. You are not equipped
With any self-indemnifying genius,
Or any sort of communal cheap armour,
Or any legend, or effete tradition,
Or native evil, to do otherwise.
He would have flown away if you had let him,

Or I know nothing of him—or of you.
Never until one morning in the spring. . . ."

"When there were trout for breakfast. Yes, I know,"
She added, sharply. "I remember them,
And I remember too, the devil's eyes
A week before in that man Umfraville.
If you must lend the devil your books to read,
Why must he bring them back when you are gone?"

"I cannot answer you when you ask that,"
He said, with half a question in his voice,
"For I am not the ruler of his kingdom.
Never until one morning in the spring,
As I was saying, did even a flicker of this
Go by my sight, almost to be forgotten
While it was going. Why should I have kept it
Before me, as you say that you have kept
The visage of a learned fisherman?
Would it have been so strange if in my folly
I should have called myself remorseful names,
And then forgotten wholly? If I know you
As once I knew you, I should hardly say so."

"You know so much of me," Gabrielle said,
With a dry languor that for Bartholow
Was like a tune that he had heard somewhere
Before, played raspingly on flattened strings,
"That I'll add nothing to your golden hoard
Of wisdom. I should only blemish it.
I'll keep the few poor farthings of my knowledge
Where they belong. You are too wise already
To let me, if I would,—and I would not—
Say even another word about that house;
And that would be in you, all by itself
A very necessary part of wisdom;
And there's one other item I commend
In your appraisal of my destitution.
I was not made for this. When you said that,
You said the best of all that was worth saying,
For which I thank you. I was not made for this.
I was a plant prepared for other soil
Than yours on which I fell; and so I've shrunk.
I'd best have withered."

            Bartholow felt once more
The shaking of her voice before it ceased,

And Gabrielle believed that his eyes changed
As if at last the ice in them were melting—
Or more as if he wished that it might melt.
She felt them searching her with a sad wonder,
That would not yet believe, or, if believing,
Would not relinquish a forsworn indulgence
Of a wrecked hope that viewed incredulously
The wreck with which it sank. If he had said
Aloud, instead of saying with his eyes
That his hard pity had become for him—
As well she knew it had—a reliquary
For a few lonely memories left of habit,
He would have told her no more than she heard.

"No, there is no long reason that I follow,"
He said, "for any longer talk of houses
That might be good for you and me to live in.
Not that it matters now, except for you.
You are not destitute, and you may build
Yourself another house, one of these days,—
One that will be away from trees and rivers,
And nearer the world's music. I was wrong
To shut you up in such a place as this,

And it was wrong of you to let me do it—
Though God knows I was far from saying so
Till you, telling me nothing, told enough
For me to hear. I heard you in the woods,
And sometimes in the moonlight by the river,
Telling yourself that you had better stayed
Nearer to your familiar streets and scenes,
As all believed you would—until you smiled,
And there was jealousy in Ascalon.
You had no right to be so beautiful,
Or I to be so blind. When I did see,
My sight was only darkness. It was wrong,
And sadly wrong, for me to go so far
Into that darkness and to take you with me,
Though I saw not where I was taking you,
Nor more where I was going. It was dark. . . .
No. I should hardly say there was a reason
For you and me to talk of houses now.
Your doubt that morning when I told of one
That I was building, as you prophesied,
More out of nothing than of anything,
Was founded more to last than any house
That you and I may build of sand on sand—

Like children I have seen down by the river.
After one tide there would be no more houses;
Only the sand again the same as ever,
The same as it is now there in the moonlight;
And as for that, the same as it is here.
There is no need of going to the river,
Either for sand or moonshine. We have both,
Here on high ground, and we have nothing else;
And when we know that we have only sand
And moonshine for a fabric, why say more
Of houses?"

        "I shall say no more of them,"
She said, and the same shaking of her lips
Came back and held her silent while she bit them
Into a short and insecure subjection
That gave her speech again: "It is not good
To say the same thing always, or to look
Too long at nothing, as we are looking now.
If I were some one else, I might see more,
For then there might be more. If I were you,
I might regain myself, as you have done,
And so persuade myself that I was going,

Like you, by endless roads into a region
Where there should be no sand. I spare your moon-
    shine,
For it may not be that. If I were wiser,
I might yet live to make myself all over,
And make you to forget me as I was
When we were here together in the darkness,
In all that I should be. This episode,
Although it fills your eyes with ice tonight
Instead of execration and hell fire,
Is only a short part of a long story
That would have been about the same without it,
And had the same conclusion. If I were lighter,
I might rise out of this and fly away
On wings a little worse for a blind singeing.
But you were right—I was not made for this;
And I was made no more, so it appears,
For that. I'm always asking why it was
That I was made. Assuredly not for you.
But why should I be tiresome, or assume
That you care, now, whether I am or not?
I'm only saying I shall soon be gone
Away from here, and you will soon be free.

As you have said, you are not going to die.
Far from it, I surmise. If I saw death
As a worse thing than your deliverance,
Awaiting you some day, from everything
Alive that was a trailing shred of me,
I'd wish to live—almost; and wholly wish it
If we could read and speak in the same language,
In the same world. You might remember that."

In the familiar turn of her last words
There was a momentary wistfulness
That pierced him as he listened, and unrolled,
In a slow gleam that faded, the long picture
Of his complacent years before the clouds
Of truth covered the light and put it out,
For a long time. "I shall remember that,"
He said, and looked into her lonely eyes
Calmly, without a vestige left in his
Of hope or hesitation. He had striven
So long to keep them cold that he foresaw
The melting down of his inclemency
Into misleading tears if he heard more
Like that. "O yes, I shall remember it,

And with it things you may not have remembered,
And some you do not know. My debt to you,
Although it may be vague, is measureless;
And the worst part of all that I am paying
Is my regret that you should have paid more.
Without you, I should not be as I am;
And as I am, or rather as we are now,
I see somewhere the progress of all roads,
Even those that in appearance have no end,
And the continuance of all works undone.
Here in this coil of our complexities
One may as well not say where roads have ends,
Or how far they are going in the darkness,
Or where we may be driven, or drive others.
Those who are led may lead, and those who lead
May follow. In the darkness all is dark.
Which, too, is vague enough."

                    "Not in the least,"
She said, pinching her lips together slowly
Before she spoke. "I see no vagueness there;
Though I could see a waste of mercy there—
But for a stranger waste of more than that,

And old as women. Some of us are changing.
But those who change the most will not change much,
And will not have to. And it's well for them
They are not all like me—and well for you;
For then you might be lonely when I'm gone.
No, I have not forgot what you were saying,
Nor could you in a lifetime be more lucid.
I am the bridge, then, over which you pass,
Here in the dark, to find a lighted way
To a new region where I cannot follow,
And where there is not either sand or moonshine,
And a new sun shines always. Well, that's something.
It may be all it was that I was worth.
'You are not worth—' you said; and then you stopped.
And I shall never know, unless you tell me,
Just what it was that I was ever worth.
Not much—or so I fear . . . Good night."

                         She rose,
And would have said no more, had he not spoken:
"I'm sorry that my tongue let loose those words,
For now I may as well as not be sorry.
With or without a cause for saying them,

They were no part of me. If you forget them,
You will have less to burden you, and less
To bear away with you. I was born here,
But I shall not die here."

                    "They're better loose
And off your tongue," she said, "if they were on it,
Waiting to be let loose. If I forget them,
I shall forget so much that a few words
Like those will hardly be as audible
Hereafter as one insect in the grass,
Where now I seem to hear a million of them.
I wonder where they go when the cold comes,
Perhaps they go to heaven." Her lips moved
And would have smiled if they had not forgotten
What they were doing. She was nearer now
And she was looking at his eyes again,
To see for the last time if there was hidden
Within them anywhere a better reason
For her to linger than to go away.
Failing, she laid her hands upon his head
And touched his forehead with her shaking lips.
"You might remember that," she said, and left him.

Not sure that she knew why it was he trembled,
Yet sure enough that it was less for her
Than for the saviour-friend who had betrayed him,
She left him, and went slowly from the room,
And slowly to the stairs. When half way up,
She paused and saw him standing at the window,
Where the moths plunged and whirred eternally,
Torn by their own salvation. She passed on,
Slowly and softly, leaving him there alone
To watch the trees, the moonlight and the river,
And to see none of them. Now in her room,
She sat for a long time in a dim silence,
Watching alone, above him, in the moonlight,
The same world he was watching there below—
Save now she could see everything out there
So clearly that she would not look at it.

She stirred at last, and with a smaller light
Put out the world and sky; and she could see
All the mute things that once had been so much
A part of her that now they all had voices,
Each whispering of a stillness in the past,
Long faded, and of other stillnesses;

And she could feel, as if a ghost had come
Between her and her worn eyes in the mirror,
The fall of the first shadow she had thrown
So long before, and so unconsciously,
Over a man's illusions and his life,
And over hers. "Yes, we are all at work,"
She thought, recalling how another man
Had branded the words on her with his eyes,
"On one another—or we may be so;
And we are least alone with our regrets
When we are most apart—or may be so;"
And so on, like a wheel blown by the wind,
Accomplishing a futile revolution
Over and over, and unceasingly,
Until a dizzy respite frightened her
And she was on her feet. With a scared glance
At one familiar object and another
She waited for the pang of intercession
That would not seize her where she stood inert,
And for the promise of a braver way
Than her earth-weary vision recognized
As hers, where there was nothing beyond earth.
And earth, she knew, had failed in her to find,

In time, the only other way there was,
Which, lying without her knowledge or her sight,
Might as well not have been—and so had not.
She with her world behind her was alone,
And he with his before him was alone—
Past all pursuit. If she pursued him now,
He would look back at her as at a stranger,
And then be gone. Cold as it was, the road
Before her would be not so cold as that.
No preparation was awaiting her
That in a moment she had not achieved.
Anything dark thrown over a white face
To make it nothing would be equipage
Complete for such a brief and shadowy journey
As hers would be down there among the trees
And memories. Now the room was gloom again,
Until a slow gleam filled it. Through the window
She saw the moon and stars, and under them
The river through the trees, and the far hills
Beyond them. All was there as it had been,
And as it was to be. She felt herself
Drawn to the door, as if a kindly ghost
Were leading her and she must follow it

Where she was led. On through a silent house
That had been too long silent she went softly,
And down another stairway she went softly,
And through another door; and there she was.
Now she could see the moon and stars again
Over the silvered earth, where the night rang
With a small shrillness of a smaller world,
If not a less inexorable one,
Than hers had been; and after a few steps,
Made cautiously along the singing grass,
She saw the falling lawn that lay before her,
The shining path where she must not be seen,
The still trees in the moonlight, and the river.

VI

FINDING himself alone there at the window,
   Bartholow scarcely knew that he had risen,
Or moved; and though the scene outside was old,
Now it appeared as new, and like to nothing
Manifest there before. And for a time,
Nothing was all there was. There were the trees,
And there was all the rest; and yet the place
That he had known was gone. The silver gleam
That gave an outline to those unreal hills
Was more the moonlight of an empty stage,
Where all was over or would soon be so,
Than of a world where men and women lived
In houses they had made. Nothing was real
That he could see, and nothing had been real
That he remembered. Gabrielle, who had gone,
Was no more real tonight than was Penn-Raven,
Who had not come. "If he had never come,

All this would not have been," Bartholow thought;
And thought again: "If he had never come,
What would have been by now?" It was his turn
To search in vain to find a buried answer
Where search itself was blind. He found himself,
Now Gabrielle was gone and there remained
No face to wrench him, sick with a cold loathing
For a salvation bought with ignominy,
And for a saviour whose invidious fee
Was hospitality that he had steeped
And poisoned with unconscionable insult
Before it was flung back. Others had met
No doubt, with as oblique indignities,
And usuries unforeseen, yet none of them
Had wrought for him of their catastrophe
An armor that would gall him less to wear
Than would offense remembered to endure.
He was alone, as they had been alone
Before him, and as many a man unborn
Would some day be alone; and while he wondered
What sort of madness might awaken in him
If there were love as well as pride at work
To rouse it into being, his new-found soul

Trembled and ached with his offended clay,
Which rapidly was over-mastering
Its reigning spirit. He was glad for love
That love was gone, or if it was not gone,
Was far enough away now and behind him,
And was enough a shadow to remain one.
If there was anywhere awaiting him
A more sufficient love than hers had been,
He would not say that he might not again
Be waiting also; and he would not say
How much or little his exacting passion
For heaven and earth together might then deserve.
But while he heard feet pounding in the distance,
There was no time for these inanities
Over an unconjectured feminine
Now less than Arethusa to the purpose;
And while he saw Penn-Raven's heavy shape
Coming along intolerably nearer,
There was no room left in him for abstractions
In which a new abhorrence had no part.
With Gabrielle before him, fabricating
Of her self-weariness and self-contempt
Her stoic swan-song of inconsequence,

Penn-Raven, though he could not be far off,
Was not so tangibly a thing alive,
Or one that was anon to be disposed of,—
As clearly now he was who came in singing,
Non ti scordar di me.

                    "Not all by chance,
My friend," he said, when he saw Bartholow;
"Not all by chance; I sing because I must.
And, as it were, intuitively in tune,
Sometimes, with the occasion. Farewell's the word.
With your expressed assurance of no urging,
I shall not wait for rain before I go.
The wiser part of me—if such a part
Wins your magnanimous acknowledgment—
Tells me at last that now my hour is near,
And that for certain I shall soon be gone.
In fine, tomorrow morning. All my goods
Will fill a more minute receptacle,
I fear, than I shall when they carry me
To my last lodging; and if half an hour
Be less than I require to strap my chattels,
Whip me away and say to all who ask,

'I never knew this man. He came to me
From nowhere, and you see him going back.'
Bartholow, I'm ineffably in debt
To you for ever. When you look at me,
I'll tell you more."

                    "Go on," Bartholow said,
Not having yet possession of an impulse
More than to listen. He had not foreseen
A prelude in this key; and while it lasted
He could see nothing but a shadowy curtain,
Whereon there was a once-remembered scene
Drawn ominously and faintly on the cloth
Of night. A sickness of irresolution,
Or more of hesitation, overcame him—
Until he knew again that if he turned
His eyes too soon, deplorable destruction
Of one or other might attend his action;
While if he saw too long the meaningless
Conceit of moonlight and tranquility
That humbled him, deplorable survival
Might by default ensue. "Go on," he said;
And as he said it he could feel himself

Inveigled nearer the abysmal verge
Of indecision, where below him lay
Unplumbed abasement. Though he might be mad,
Better be mad with pride alive in him,
He thought, than be an imbecile without it;
Or so it was that a vindictive remnant
Of hitherto subservient cave-man
Persuaded or enforced him to believe.
Meanwhile a furtive curiosity
Would soon be sated with Penn-Raven's lies.
"Go on," he said once more. "I can admire
This infinite ancestral view of mine
And hear unhindered with it all you say.
Surely we know each other well enough
Not always to be talking with our faces.
When we are in the dark we do not see
Each other's faces; yet we go on talking,
As if our faces were no more of us
Than unsuccessful ornaments of nature—
Better concealed, if we are to have friends.
If we must have them, or believe we must,
I'd recommend the putting out at once
Of all our eyes. Then we should have a world

Only a little darker than it is
Tonight, and one less hazardous—may be."

"You have an amiable inventiveness
Against your friends this evening, Bartholow,"
Penn-Raven answered. His uncertainty
Jarred a long silence like an oboe blown
By a strong novice with a reed too thin
For secure volume. "If you are in the dark,—"
And there he paused. "If you are in the dark,
Let us have light. Let us have light at once,
But let us not at once put out our eyes;
For now it is we need them. Bartholow,
Your mask and its remote advantages
Are unbecoming and uncomfortable.
I can see that. Yet if it humors you
To wear the thing till you are weary of it,
Your native and superfluous privilege,
I grant you, is to wear it—if you will.
Indeed, I cannot easily remove it,
Not having, or I fear so, proper craft
Or safe intelligence to pluck it off
Without offense or pain. Tomorrow morning,

As you have heard me say before, I vanish;
The time comes always for our vanishing;
And we who know best when the time has come
Are best remembered after we are gone.
I was already well apprised of this
Before you mentioned waiting for that rain,
Which may be long arriving, and then left me—
With something enigmatic in your words
And in your silky way of saying them.
If your way was a foil of courtesy
For mine of a somewhat abrupt assumption,
We may as well go back. When I surprised you—
For so I must have done—by suddenly
Confronting your impeccable composure
With my conjecture, I was seeing pictures,
And wishing then that you for your well-being
Might have been seeing a few of them also.
There were some names that I had for them then,
But now they are not worth your recollection.
Tradition, was it? Shipwreck? Anchorage?
Give once a name to a thing best without it,
You clip the wings and bell the neck of it;
And that which was itself, and self-secure,

Becomes imprisoned, crippled, false, and common.
The picture that you see now in the moonlight
Is not one that is waiting for a name;
And all the years there are for you to live,
Now you are born, are not for you to waste
In railing at unanswerable Fate,
Who has no ears. Setting it rather sharply,
You married the wrong woman—as a few,
By competent report, have done before you,
And will be doing always, or as long
As there are men and women to be married.
When time is older, men and women wiser,
Tradition less a tyrant, and shipwreck
No more a sacrament, we'll do all this
Better—or worse—but with a difference,
Undoubtedly. The way now for you two,—
Together, I mean—comes to a quiet end.
You see it, for this moonlight is not fog,
And pride is not an anchor that will hold you
Long from the rocks. The picture that I saw
Before you left was one of a bad storm,
With faces in it that I recognized—
As long as they were there; for presently

There were no faces, and there was no picture.
Not even the ship was there. It was all fancy,
And will be nothing worse if you steer well.
A voyage may have an end without a wreck,
As yours will have unless you make the moon
Your sun to sail by. You will not do that."

Bartholow meanwhile, hearing of all this
No more than a few intermittent words
That flew at him as vainly as outside
The moths were plunging always at his window,
Had been observing a sufficient wreck
Where neither ship nor sea was requisite
To make a picture with two faces in it.
He would not see it, see it though he must—
As he must know that one of them was now
In the same room with him. If once he turned
His eyes to see it, all to come then would come—
As the primeval in him willed it should,
Even as it willed anon that he should turn them,
And then himself. Slowly, inevitably,
And with a confidence unfortified
Except with an oblivious disregard

Of soiled regrets or mortal consequence,
He went a few steps forward, and then paused
With a few more to go. Now he could see
The solemn questioning in the other's eyes,
And in the living fire that he had found
So many a time behind them he could read
Composure worse than hate. "Damn you, Penn-
     Raven,"
Bartholow said, securely and distinctly;
And, with a poise that was almost a leisure,
Came a step nearer. But he saw no change
In the white, heavy face, or the calm eyes,
Or the calm fire behind them. For an instant
A flinching sadness may have clouded them,
But only once, if then; and if at all,
It came and went unseen by Bartholow,
Who merely said once more, "Damn you, Penn-
     Raven."
Everything else that he had meant to say,
Or would have wished there might have been to say,
Was lost in a sick blur. Whether he struck
Before he leapt, or leapt before he struck,
He knew not. He did not know anything—

Until he felt Penn-Raven's heavy shape
Beneath him on the floor, and his thick neck
Luxuriously yielding to his fingers,
Which felt their way to death, or might have done so,
But for the shock of an abrupt upheaval
After which all was dark. When there was light
He saw, from the same chair where he had sat
With Gabrielle before him in another,
The sad eyes of his adversary gazing
Calmly and patiently down into his,
And felt the crushing of two iron hands
Upon his aching arms.

         "Well, Bartholow,"
Penn-Raven said, smiling unhappily,
"Your speed, if not your zeal, was unexpected;
And you have in you more of your grandfather
Than first one had imagined. You have done it,
And in a fashion done it rather well.
These aboriginal necessities
Of yours have had, we'll hope, an adequate
Eruption and release; and this achieved,
You're fit now for an action more serene

And for an energy more temperate.
Next time you are not likely to do more,
Or quite so much—unless, improbably,
I find that I have let you go too soon,
And with a faith too sure. So there you are,
With nothing broken in you but your pride,
Which happily will heal itself again—
Though I hope not the sooner for this onslaught;
For I can see in that no more to praise,
Or blame, than a familiar atavism,
By no means yours alone. If we consider
The many that have been alive to make us,
And are so many parts of each of us,
The qualified assent of our perception
Will hardly measure either up or down,
I fear, exclusively to our illusions.
Wherefore, if I exact of you your word
Of honor—and your word will be enough—
I'll trust you to be seated as you are,
And to extinguish all those hesitations
That linger in your eyes. Your desk, I think,
Is locked; and I would rather leave it so.
You do not want my death-wound on your soul,

Or my unpleasant carcass on your floor;
Yet having in my tangled heritage
A thread of elementary suspicion,
I see no instant reason to forget
That you have shown me, among other treasures,
A more pernicious and ingenious pop-gun
Than elsewhere I've admired. Now if your word
Of honor failed you, or if you forgot it,
And, so reduced, you made an end of me
By stealthy and unworthy agencies,
Your loss would not be mine; and your reward
Would be but one unwholesome smoky moment
Over the coarse and least implicit part
Of all that makes up me. Whether it die
Tonight or half a century from tonight,
The rest of me may know so little of it
As maybe not to care. One or one more,
Or fewer, of its ephemeral extensions
Made shorter for your sake would hardly serve
To make you any happier than you are;
And you are not so happy as you will be
When all this other smoke that's choking you
Shall blow away and I shall be gone with it.

You may as well sit there where you are now
As walk about, though I shall not molest you
If walk about you must and will. That's wiser—
For you'll be none too agile or alert
For a time yet. I shall go presently,
And in the morning I shall go for ever—
Or naturally at once, if you insist;
Though I shall be inveterately beholden
To you and your attention if I stay
Around the clock again. All which implies,
I hope, a friendly reticence—and, I trust,
A humane brevity."

                        "I have no means,"
Bartholow answered from his chair, "to move you,
Or not without assistance or a scene
As long if not as noisy as the first;
And as your manner says you are not going
Without one or the other, you may stay—
That is if insult, given and received,
Is milk and honey for you, and the breath
Of life. If I had known you were a giant,
As well as a damned parasite and a thief,

I might have shot you and been sorry for it.
To pay so much as that for such a thing
As you would be to nurse the devil's blister.
I do not want your slaughter on my soul,
Or your unpleasant carcass on my floor.
As much as that, I heard; and that was true.
If there's an idiom that will undulate
Across your meditation less obscurely
Than mine, you might announce another cue
For me to follow; or, you might get out."

Penn-Raven looked up slowly from the floor,
And with a frown of one annoyed and sorry
More than of one offended and dismissed,
Stared solemnly with his large violet eyes
At Bartholow, who found in them again
The same unfathomable innocence
That many a time before had made him smile
As with a kindly wonder. When he spoke,
His voice was that of a tragedian
Resuming after a subdued alarm
The lines of an unhappy narrative
Unfolding a mysterious history.

"All who have lived," he said, "living at all,
Must have encountered incongruities
Tangled as yours are to your contemplation—
If not, as yours are, to be shaken soon,
Untangled, and untied. Your few last knots
That in your fever are tonight so many,
Are not so many; and you are only one.
Whereas, if there were any way to count them,
Those who are struggling with more knots than yours,
And worse, would make a nation. Bartholow,
There was a man once who believed himself
Nearer to God, and by the way of reason—
Where few may see, or seeing may dare to go—
Than all the martyrs by the way of faith.
Now, I am not so sure that he was there—
Though I believe it; and if I believe it,
For all my needs I know it. Yes, he was there;
And where he was, he is,—a little scarred
Tonight, but nowhere else than where he was.
There is no going back from such a place—
Or not by the same road; yet there are pits
Along the way, and there are darknesses,
As on all other ways—only far deeper,

And, after an excess of blinding light,
Unconscionably darker. It is well
For him and his humility, I doubt not,
That all should be as obviously it is
Along that way; for he might otherwise find,
With restless and impetuous feet, like yours,
A darker path leading him back again
Where the old road that others had not seen
Might not be seen again, even by him;
And though it might be seen, might not be taken.
All the forgotten sights of infancy—
Which far outlives the cradle—though at first
A burden, would be no long time becoming
Endurable and as easy as before,
Putting out slowly the one sight that sees.
You are not there, and you are not to go there;
Though pride, that eminent adjunct of the devil,
May keep a dwindling sort of regency
Over the rule of your protesting wisdom,
For certain days. You are not going back,
Yet as one mortal to another mortal—
Each in appearance and unhappy proof
Still fallible—I'll imagine that you might.

You are still coiling your credulity
Around you like a snake that would be glad
If only you would let him go away
Before he has to bite you any more;
And that's not either love or bravery
In you, and the snake knows it. Let him go.
Love at its wildest has, if it be love,
A reticence and a sort of dignity
That passion, with pride always urging it
Along to the old wreck in the old storm,
Will not acknowledge or not unwillingly
Regard or recognize. Love, it is true,
May wear the stain of pride and still be love,
And on occasion irretrievably
Say more than should be told—and to no end
Than to sow fennel and regret where flowers
Too rare for the gratuity of a name
Were not to live . . . were not to live." He ceased,
And looked away as if he had forgotten
All he had said before so fluently;
And then he said, as with a slow remorse
That dragged a melancholy after it,
"Were not to be."

              Bartholow, still aware
That a few words of his if he should say them,
Or his departure without saying them,
Would soon enough accomplish an escape,
Sat waiting, an indignant and chagrined
Prisoner of his curiosity.
A vision of thick lips and violet eyes
Oppressed him, though the eyes were looking down
And the face mostly hidden by the hand
That covered them, till a more solemn pause
Than in the circumstances he could share
Galled him again to speech.   "Well, what's the matter?
There are no flowers now in your garden? Well,
You never told me that you had a garden.
You may, then, like an apt and able blackguard,
Have torn away on someone else's fence
The friendly cloak of lies that you have worn
So long over that shrunken soul of yours.
Easy mistakes are common in the dark,—
Notably so where there are friends together;
And you, with your cheap fennel and regret,
And your sweet compound of hypocrisy,
Are worse than common dirt. I like to say this;

And if your notion is to break my neck
For saying it, I'm not sure that I shall care.
When a man's last illusion, like a bubble
Covered with moonshine, breaks and goes to nothing,
And after that is rather less than nothing,
The bubble had then better be forgotten
And the poor fool who blew it be content
With knowing he was born to be a fool.
As we are born to be, apparently,
So are we; and it's well for most of us
We do not know too soon. We know too late.
Well, what's the matter? Has your spring of lies
Dried up—or is it almost full again?"

"Forgive me if I do not always listen,"
Penn-Raven answered. There was hesitation
More than uncertainty in his approach,
And there was disappointment and impatience
At first in his returning innocence,
Now master of his eyes and of the man
Who gazed unwillingly into their calm
And solemn fire. "Forgive me, Bartholow;
Your dreams have taken you so far from home

That I must wait for an awakening,
Or by degrees induce it. If I do,
You may be learning less reluctantly
How far you are from here, where there is nothing
To hold you any longer. For a time
There was a woman who was never here,
And it was your misguided quest of her,
Where she was not, that led you to the shadows,
And nearer to the tomb than either you
Or she, or rather your sad fiction of her,
Had wisdom to conceive. There was a man,
Also; and though far distant and unsought,
He was already on his way to save you,
Albeit he was untold and unaware
Of your disaster or your need of him.
Nothing between Arcturus and the earth
Is there more surely or insolubly
Than these things that are so. There was a man
On whom a light fell once, as once a light
Fell sharp on Saul—though it was not like that;
Or possibly it was. There are these things,
And they are so—until we give them names,
And harness them with words that have one meaning

For no two men; and likelier none at all
For one man—or one woman.   Now and again
There may be one to pass on to another
A living torch that others cannot see—
And all should then be well; and would have been,
Even here and in this house, if in this man,
Who came because a will not his compelled him,
Fear and a fearful hope had faded out
Before there was a fire.   There was no place
Under the stars, he thought, where love was more
Than love had always been: not everything,
Yet no small matter, even under the stars.
And there was in his armor, so he thought,
No rift—until he found there was no armor
Against a love that he had long abjured
As one that would be kinder for not coming.
Sure that his house that was not made with hands
Was built forever, he was too sure to see;
And you are not seeing so much tonight, I fear,
As your destructive and incensed endeavor
Never to see again is hiding from you.
Yet I see little in this that's ominous,
For your endeavor is only transitory,

And your destruction is less imminent
Than mine was lately in a way to be,
And would have been if like you I had heard
The call of our inferior forbears
To grievous action or infirm despair.
Not that I should have murdered anybody,
Or put myself away, and so undone
Deliriously my work not yet achieved,—
Although, not being beyond mortality,
I might abjectly have capitulated
As you did—not for pride, but worse than that:
I might have yielded, after disillusion,
To go the desolate way of doubt again.
There may be somewhere in forgotten song
A love like mine, though hardly quite another
In life, I fancy; for so it seems to me,
And so to me it is—or so it was.
Was, is, or may be always—let it fade;
Or if it will die sometime, let it die.
There are some ills that sooner will be dead
For our not vexing them with remedies;
And there are some that have their remedies
In their remedial evil. Let them fade;

[137]

And if they will die sometime, let them die.
Meanwhile our occupation is to live,
And somehow to be wiser for a woman
Who, as we thought, was here; and was not here."

Bartholow's face, by this time slowly drawn
With anger and accumulating wonder
Into a tortured smile, suddenly fell
Into his hands; and his whole body shook
With a malevolent and indecent laughter
That ended in a sort of toiling moan,
Like that of a man strangling. "Oh, my God!"
He groaned, still shaking. But he said no more,
And only after a torn interval
Of revelation did his ears avouch
A furtive acquiescence and surrender.
Call himself what he might, his only choice
Was to be lashed with a fanatic whip
That left upon him now hardly a welt.
All this was for the moment understood,
Partly to be forgotten, partly scorned,
And wholly for a season to be crushed
And sunken, like a piece of yielding earth

Compelled inevitably and impossibly
To be a fulcrum for too many forces.

"Well, if you like it, laugh," Penn-Raven said;
And there was the same anxious innocence
In the large eyes that gazed on Bartholow,
Who now looked at him with a weary scorn
Whereon there yet remained a cloudy smear
Of his inclement mirth. "Yes, if you like it.
I cannot say I like the sound of it;
And for your sake I'll hope no more of it
Is in you to be rankling a way out;
And there my fears are brief. You are not one
To steep a needless poison with another,
Bitter enough without it, and then swallow
The whole perfidious dose to no effect
Than to be sicker than you were before.
You are not one to fling yourself alive
Among wolves, hoping unworthily thereby
To be devoured at once without a fight
On your side to be free. You are not one,
Because a woman has with eyes not yours
Looked on a world not yours and now not hers,

To say that all worlds are as insubstantial
As a dream world of hers, or yours, or mine,
May once have been. You are not one to flout
The power of all your services unseen
That soon you are to see, and are to give,
When really you conceive yourself alive.
You that have heretofore not seen or served
Are surely by some worthier subterfuge
Than this to fling the dust of one illusion
Over the chariot wheels of destiny
Into the eyes of truth. You are not one
To do all this because the flower you thought
Was love you found the fairest of all weeds
That ever bloomed alone where there were shadows.
For you it was no more than that; for me
It was *la bella donna assoluta;*
Though for itself, and in a proper garden,
It might not have been either; and for you
After a time, not much in any event.
You found it blooming in a lonely place
Where the sun touched it only to revive it
For new endurance of another day
That was like all before; and being yourself

A gardener more adept in admiration
Than in selection, brought it home with you,
And to a darker loneliness than ever,
And there it might have withered for the sun
That would have saved it, and so might have died;
But something of the weed was in it still,
And in its northern grace there was a taint,
Or may have been one, of a tropic languor.
We do not have to go so far as that
For the unseen survivals that are in us—
As your inimical activities
Have demonstrated. Put the surest of us
Too far beyond the boundaries of our nature,
And we shall be the last who are to say
Just what rebellions and indifferences
May thwart or poison us. We cannot know.
And if, like her, we see beyond ourselves
Nothing, what have we then within ourselves
Worth seeing or worth saving? She may live
To wither and to fade and be forgotten
Or there may be awaiting her somewhere
On earth another garden far from here.
A miracle may reveal to her denial

Color and light that will not be denied;
And she may live to see. If such a garden
Be not awaiting her—well, you have heard:
She fades, and withers. Were she more a weed,
She might be all a weed. But she's not that—
Being flower and weed together, as we have seen.
Who shall say more of her? Not you, not I.
She may go soon—even here, before you know it.
Or she may not go soon. She may be old
Before she goes—though earth has little need
Of her allegiance to it. There is earth
Enough, and there will always be enough,
For you and me without her. She may go
So soon that you will hardly be aware
Of more than a weed sickled in the night
To shrivel in the sun; or, miracles yet,
And other gardens, may be still on earth
Awaiting her. I do not see them now,
Yet they may be. There are these things that are;
And here are we among them. Is it well,
Or is it ill, that we be where we are,—
Here, and among them? Be it well or ill,
Your doom now is to see, and see alone.

Whether she go tomorrow or tonight,
Or live on to fade out and be forgotten
Is now for you no matter—or for me.
I do not ask you for your gratitude,
Nor for your word that you are free. If that
Were branded with an iron across your forehead,
I should not read it any clearer there
Than on a living page that I see now
Before me in a volume that is you.
Your doom is to be free. The seed of truth
Is rooted in you, and the fruit is yours
For you to eat alone. You cannot share it,
Though you may give it, and a few thereby
May taste of it, and so not wholly starve.
Thank me or not, there is no other way;
And there is no road back for you to find.
And she . . . she is not either yours or mine."

Bartholow, writhing, licked his lips and waited,
As if to leap again before he spoke.
But leaping, as he reasoned, would be folly,
And speech, if he remained, humiliation.
Yet there he must remain till he might rise

Of his own will and go away. The fear
Of death would not have held him as he was;
But there he was, and he was held. "Go on,"
He said; "I may as well have heard you out
Before you go out. When you go, you go;
And you are going soon."

            Penn-Raven frowned
As he had frowned before, as one annoyed
More than as one dismissed, and having sighed,
Said on: "She is not either yours or mine.
The ruins at last have crushed her; and she knows
At last that they were ruins before they fell.
And if she pushed a few of them away,
I am not sure that she has in her now
Power enough to lift the rest of them,
Or pride enough to care if they were lifted.
Negation is a careless architect,
Doomed always to be crushed or maimed somehow
In the undoing and the falling down
Of its own house. If a kind ignorance
Had shielded her from seeing how sure it was
To fall, it might have spared her the false toil

Of building in the dark. Her tragedy
Is knowing how hard it is to care so little
For all that is unknown, and heed so little
Of all that is unseen. She made herself
Believe she loved the world that wearied her
Until she left it and saw what it was,
Unwillingly, that she was not to see.
She learned of you on your awakening
What she was not to see, and she saw nothing.
Today she will not let herself believe
She cares whether or not there's anything
Worth caring for. The soul in her is frozen,
Where yours was only sick. She plays with lies,
Knowing them to be lies, and humors them
The more because she is afraid of them
The most when they are friendly. But for knowledge,
Glowering always and invisibly
Before her like a shadowy sort of tiger,
She might assume a strength to raise herself
Again to look back at the chilly world
That you have taken from her; and if then
Should be the tiger's time to spring at her—
Well, there are wilder things awaiting us,

And worse, than tigers. But she knows her world
Too well to carry there a frozen soul
To warm at those false fires. She would go on
With you, if there were such a way for her,
But she would not be with you very long,
Or to more purpose than to know as much
Of you and of herself as now she knows
Too late—which is enough."

              "Yes, quite enough,"
Bartholow said. Deaf to the mystic fervor
That once had healed and liberated him
With its immortal implications,—now,
Like a betrayed apostate, he could hear
Nothing in speech or prophecy but sound.
And while he heard he wondered why it was
That he must listen when there was a door
But a few steps away, and a whole house,
Not mentioning a world, where he might hear
No more of this. "Yes, it is quite enough—
Of her. There is no more for you to say
Of her, unless your pleasure be to say it
Here to yourself alone."

"Your careful scorn
Is not unwarranted by circumstance,"
Penn-Raven answered. "It will do no harm
Tonight, and it will do no good tomorrow.
If you believe that all you found is lost,
And that you too are struggling among ruins,
You are not long for your belief. Your dawn
Is coming where a dark horizon hides it,
And where a new day comes with a new world.
The old that was a place for you to play in
Will be remembered as a man remembers
A field at school where many victories
Were lost in one defeat that was itself
A triumph over triumph—now disowned
In afterthought. You know as well as I
That you are the inheritor tonight
Of more than all the pottage or the gold
Of time would ever buy. You cannot lose it
By gift or sale or prodigality,
Nor any more by scorn. It is yours now,
And you must have it with you in all places,
Even as the wind must blow. I cannot say
All that I would, for you have ears tonight

Only for words; and when they are no more
Than language, our best words are mostly nothing.
The wiser way for you is to forget them
Until you cease to fear them. You have played
With life as if it were a golden toy,
Till you believe that you have shattered it.
Tomorrow you will see that you have not.
In honor of your wish I'll say no more
Of her that I shall see no more. I failed
With her, as you did; and now she has failed.
Tomorrow . . . but we'll say no more of her;
It is your wish."

                    "For God's sake, go away!"
Bartholow rose, and would have gone himself,
Had not a subtle inspiration stayed him
While he prepared with a malignant zeal
One final insult. "When you go," he said,
"And you are going soon, you may require
Assistance on your way out of my sight.
With your permission I'll arrange a means
To insure a swifter and a safer distance
Between us than your leisure might achieve

On your resource alone. A cheque will do it—
And there you have it. Do not hesitate,
For if you do your pantomime will only
Be one more lie; and you have lied enough
And stolen enough. Something in you is true,—
I know that; and I know that all the rest
Will be a small and rotten residue
For you to contemplate before you die.
If I were you, and were the parting guest,
I should not ask for more. You'll find this ample
For the removal of what you yourself
Denominate as your unpleasant carcass.
Take it, and now—get out of this!"

                  Penn-Raven,
Having observed the cheque attentively,
Stood holding it until with absent care
He folded it and put it in his pocket.
"Thank you," he said. "You are magnanimous,
Being so from birth. As your ferocity
Misled you but a little while ago,
Now in its turn your magnanimity
Prevails. There are small fellows everywhere

Who might not, as I do, dismiss the whim
You think your motive, and so be assured,
As I am, that you are not one of them.
Pity them, if you will, but never mind them,
Even while you serve them; for you are to serve
Henceforth as one may serve who is alive
Among so many that are not alive.
If they were yet alive, why should they play
So hard at living, leaving at the end
Only a few regrets for having played
No harder? There's a pathos here in this;
For all must yet be done by the unborn
And by the dead together before life
May know itself to be alive. The few
Who see, see this; and you are one of them,
Although tonight a cloud is hiding you
From your soul's eye. I do not ask of you
Your gratitude, or question any method
Your purpose entertains—though I may ask
Whether perchance obscure appearances
May or may not attend my too abrupt
Departure to the town, where we are known
Rather as friends, I fancy. There's a train

Away at midnight, but there's never sleep
For me on wheels and rails."

                    Bartholow stared,
And then threw up his hands in helplessness.
"Damn you, and your obscure appearances!
Get out. I'll send your traps on after you,
Into the town, or back again to nowhere—
All as you may direct. And now—get out!"

Penn-Raven, hesitating, bowed his head,
Like one subdued by doubt. When he looked up
His eyes were those of an offended child
Wherein reproof and stricken innocence
Were seen through shining tears that were too much
For Bartholow's abused credulity.
Unwilling or unfit to trust himself
Again to speech, he said it in one look;
And then, turning his back upon his guest,
He moved away slowly towards the window
Where the same moths were flying at the screen
And there was the same moonlight. So he stood,
And so Penn-Raven stood, without a word,
Gazing at Bartholow regretfully,

And with no anger in his violet eyes.
His thick lips and his large white iron hands
Were trembling, but there was no fury in them
For Bartholow's attention had he seen them;
Although it may have been as well for both
That neither saw the other's face again
Until there was a crunch of rushing feet
Outside along the gravel, and anon
The sound of a slow knocking at the door.

VII

AFTER this night, and yet another night,
     There was a knocking on another door
Where none till now had ever come so early,
And few at any time, early or late;
Wherefore it was with mingled injuries
That Umfraville, the learned fisherman,
Like an unhappy turtle pushed his head
Slowly out of the cover that enclosed him,
Listening while his miscreated face
Became awake. There was another knocking
Hurried and hard, at which he growled and rose,
Yawning and inly cursing whatsoever
Untimely and unseemly visitant
The door might hide until he opened it.
He opened it, and there was Bartholow—
Pallid and changed, and calm.

[153]

                    "I know your ways,"
He said at once, abruptly, while his eyes,
Pathetic with unwonted hesitancy
And a constrained humility, said more;
"I know your ways and hours, and therefore owe
Your patience my apologies. Forgive me,
For I have learned that you of all my friends,
Who are not half so many as they would seem,
Are the securest and the best worth having.
This have I learned of late, and rather strangely.
I could have said that you had told me so,
Across the river—almost when it happened."

The learned hermit, gradually aware,
Though sleepily, of what his friend was saying,
Pushed wide the door, and Bartholow came in.
"I have been here alone and have heard nothing,"
Said Umfraville, who, robed in white and brown,
Was now more like a zebra than a scholar.
"So it has happened—has it? Wait a little,
And I'll hear more—or no. Your tongue is yours.
I knew you might be coming here sometime—
Like this—one of these days. Or I believed
                    [154]

I knew it. Being a student, I foresaw
The possible. Now for God's sake have a chair."
With that, he stretched and yawned and disappeared,
Leaving his guest alone in a gray light
Where there was only books that few could read
In any light. Bartholow looked at them,
But they were all asleep and they said nothing
More than a mouldy whisper of the past.

After a mighty splashing, Umfraville
Appeared again, arrayed in shopworn hues
Unsalable, at which another man
Than Bartholow this morning would have smiled.
"So it has happened," he began again.
"Well, I supposed it would; and longer since
Than I have seen you have I been supposing—
When I've had fancies. 'What's it all to me?'
I've asked myself; and yet, you being friendly—
Well, I've had fancies. While you found your soul,
I found your reason for the need of one;
Or so believed. I hope you have it with you;
For surely it would be a scurvy soul
To fail you now; that is, if what has happened

Is what apparently was happening.
There are the wise, and you are one of them,
Meanwhile, to know your friend and seek him out.
God made a sorry mess of his appearance,
But here he is, and as he is you have him.
Another man, we'll fancy, might have less
In having none soever to seek out;
But that's a fancy. Have they gone together,
Or has that bland and sainted scalawag,
Your saviour, gone with half your patrimony?
I warned you long ago that I'm a growth
Not loved in your clipped world; and I've a speech,
I fear, that may offend in friendliness
Till we've had some hot coffee. Even so,
You know that you have come to the right place
At the right time; and that's a deal of knowledge.
Before I let you talk I'll warm the works;
For mortal engines are inadequate
Except we give them fuel— by your leave."

Bartholow, silent, sat abstractedly
Observing his uncouth and frog-like host
At some superfluous early occupation,

Which partly was a vague metallic noise
That he could hear, and partly a vain motion
That would some day be stopped like a machine
That walked and fussed and fumbled and wore clothes
Too strange to cover life. He thought of that
Until he saw the world a spinning cinder,
Where neither fire nor pride would burn again,
Or be remembered. Then a steamful odor
Filled him, and he could hear a voice that said
Something about a cup that would not pass
Until he drank it . . .

       "You have done well, so far,"
Said Umfraville at last. "You could not eat,
Yet somehow you have eaten. You could not say
What most it was that you were here to say,
Yet somehow you have said as much of it
As need be said. You have done well, so far;
You have done well to tell me how she died,
But ill to tell me that you know not why.
You may say nothing, and within your right
Of silence have an end of my remarks
At any time when a word wearies you

Or scratches you, but you are not to say—
To me, at least—that you see mysteries
Among the reasons why she drowned herself.
You may say she was free to understand
That all was over, and that she was free
Thereafter to go flitting her own way
To whatsoever shades or lights or fires
There might be waiting and alluring her,
But surely you will do your tongue the honor
Not to pretend again that you believe it
When it says that to me—for I'm a student.
We readers of the dead are not so blind
That we see nothing that is not behind us."

Bartholow crossed his fingers, twisting them
In a confused uncertainty. "I believe
That I have told you everything but one thing,
Too near for telling. There's a warning humor
That waits even on the dead, and will protect them.
God knows that I would do no less for them—
For her, at least. Yet rather would I say it
Than be the creature of your inferences.
It is a common process, for that matter,

Whereby a change that once was unforeseen
Is born too late.   When all was wrecked and ended,
I might, if I had been some other man,
Have had the remnant that was left of her
To cherish unto death.   But how was that
To be, seeing I was no other man
Than he that is before you.   There was talk,
On my side, of a new house we should build
Together—yet I knew the while I talked
That I was only talking; for I knew
There was no house to build.   I'll not affront
The old funereal decencies by saying
More now than I have said.   I don't forget
That she is lying cold there where I left her,
Or that when I go back there I shall find her.
There was a madness that was born with her,
And I am not her judge."

                    "There may have been,"
Said Umfraville, "a madness born with her—
Quite as you say.   Quite as you say, indeed.
There is a madness born with all of us,
Possibly.   There are signs enough of it.

No longer time ago than half a minute
I should have said again that I believed
You knew; but I believe now that you don't.
The poisoning inertia of our custom
Has had its way with many a man before,
And many a woman. She who died of it
That night, if so she died, was only one;
And you, who are alive in spite of it,
Are only one. Your saviour may have saved you,
But never fancy now that in your freedom
Your fee is paid. Your freedom is itself
Another poison, or may turn to one
If you consume too much of it. Your soul
May shrink, if you are too familiar with it,
To such offended and obscure concealment
That you may never find it in this life
Again—assuming always, or for now,
That you have found it. Something you have found,
I grant you, but a benison to beware
And to be wary of, and to respect
As you respect your senses—reasonably.
As for your friend, you've seen enough of him
In seeing him on his way out of your sight.

You have enough of him in his achievement.
If a true artist must go to the devil,
What's left of truth in him should keep the devil
Out of his art; whereas if your true seer
Must be a liar for variety,
He'll soon see double. And on the other hand,
Strange bottles hold God's wine, or we are told so.
And I believe old sayings, for I'm a student.
You have a choice of ambiguities."

Bartholow rose, and having risen, he smiled
A little with his lips at Umfraville.
"I should have hardly come to you," he said,
For such an early douche of rudiments.
Illuminations are all dangerous
If we are too familiar with our fires,
You say; and though I might have drawn as much
As that from my own well, I'm not ungrateful.
I thank you, for I know you are my friend;
And I'll apologize eternally
For stirring you at such a vicious hour.
My coming is of itself an evidence
That I'm a trifle shaken, as you see."

"Only a trifle," said the fisherman;
"And a few rudiments will do no harm.
Sit down. Now as for these illuminations,
The world is always dark when they go out;
And yours would be the blackest of all worlds
Without your new-found light—well nigh as black
And unendurable as hers, may be.
You thought yourself alone; and all the time
The two of you were stifling there together,
Each having wrought so long upon the other
In silence that in speech you played with lies,
Fearing a thunderbolt if truth were spoken.
I question if you need reproach the past
For those indigenous injuries of custom;
And on the chance of trampling in the fields
Of more than my domain, which is not large,
I doubt if you need pity her for the end
She made. If my conviction tells as much
Of her eclipse as your renascence tells
Of yours, you cannot wish her for your sake,
And surely not for hers, with you again
On earth; for she was dead before she died."

"You mean then that I killed her? Is it so?"
Bartholow was a long time pondering
Before he spoke again. "It may be so.
Yet, when I left her there, could she have been
So peaceful? Have the dead a special kindness
For those who kill them? I can imagine so."
He scanned again the cold unanswering books
About him, and then gazed at Umfraville
Impassively: "You believe then that I killed her?
It may be so—though I should hardly say so."

The scholar clamped his jaws together slowly,
And sighed and shook his head before he spoke:
"Since neither of you knew what you were doing
When you were groping there alone together,
You will not add a cubit to your stature
Imagining you did this or you did that.
No doubt there are some extant vulgar cynics
Who'd say that she has won. I'm only saying
The race is over; and, to use your words,
I'm not the judge. I think, if I were you,
I'd be so facile as to leave all that
To custom, the arch-enemy of nature.

Nature is here apparently to suffer,
And we who are supreme in mercy, scope,
And vision, have never failed to do our part.
How many do the sweetest of our species
Conceive they may have killed, or worse than killed?
What wreckage have the gentlest of us left
Among those who have smiled and are forgotten?
What untold inward searing of the strong
Has been the jest of innocence and weakness?
What ugliness and emptiness of change
Has been the aftermath of silly triumph?
What stings of unforgetting recollection
Have been the wages of unworldly prudence?
How many a sickening wrench of hard belief
Has been the sport of a soft egotism?
What smeared ends of unfinished histories
Are in the chronicles of disillusion?
Having a face no man may gaze upon—
Saving an only friend who doesn't see it—
I may have made you fancy I see nothing;
And I'd be willing I should see no more,
Sometimes.   There woke within me such a thought
As that when first I met your mendicant

Exotic soul-practitioner, Penn-Raven.
If it was he that saved you and redeemed you,
There was a great deal in you to be saved—
Or there was parlous little. Being your friend,
Also a student, it's an easy flight
To fancy there was much. You are soon to know,
For in the other event your light will fade
Before the crocuses are out again.
There is a voice that says it will not fade—
Though I'm not sure that one has need to hear it,
Or that it says your freedom, of itself,
May not be light enough. I cannot say
With your authority what it is that happens
When men that are themselves their prisoners
Go free again. I say, God help the women,
When they have only their own hearts to eat.
A man will eat another's and not know it,
And so conserve his own. So may a woman,
If she have one at hand that's appetizing,
And not so tough that she be weary of it.
Sometimes I have a robust apprehension
That if we were all honest cannibals,
And not such anthropophagous hypocrites,—

If we should feed on one another frankly,
And with no cloud of custom in the way
Of clarity and advancement,—we should climb
Higher than yet we are, with all the bones
Of all the weak beneath us. Never infer
From this that I approach the personal—
For I'm but an offscouring of the sphere
To which I am still clinging, for no reason
Except that I still cling. I've no illusion
That I have license to be personal
Beyond your problem—which is now not one
For you to pore on too remorsefully.
The more you make it visible, your position
Becomes a puzzlement and a devilment,
More than a desolation. In your heart
You are not sorry that your sybarite,
Your Ishmaelite, your omphalopsychite,
Or what the devil else he may have been,
Is on the road again to his next haven—
Which may, I trust, be far ahead of him.
Not even with his extortions are you sorry
That you are now alone, with no conceit

Or purpose to pursue him.   Are you sure
That he is not still here?"

                        Bartholow gazed
Out through a dusty window at the river,
As if he had not heard.   "Yes, I am sure,"
He said, indifferently.   "He is not here.
He went away.   But he would not have gone
If I had let him stay.   He would have seen
Her face once more, he said.   He did not see it.
He told me that obscure appearances
Would be remarked if he went suddenly;
But he went—suddenly.   I did not see
Her face till yesterday.   We brought her home,
And there she is.   I have not slept since then.
I have not slept these two nights now; not since
Two men came in the moonlight to my door.
They saw it from that vessel anchored there.
They saw it in the moonlight.   They could see
No other house than mine on the west side,
And they came there.   I have not slept since then;
And I may not sleep yet—for a long time.
Why should I sleep, when you say that I killed her?"

"Suppose we say to that that I said nothing,"
Suggested Umfraville, deliberately.
"As I'm a scholar and a fisherman,
I have said nothing half so venomous
As half you say I've said. You are more racked
And clubbed, as I see now, than I believed;
So I forswear all ambiguities
And once again refer your case to custom.
You keep yourself so well within yourself
That you are likely to conceal your needs
When more than ever they should be revealed.
Your world's way, doubtless, and the way of custom.
But I'm a dweller of another world,
Where all my friends are shadows—who, if here,
Alive, would only wonder what they met
If they met me. My way among my kind—
If such a kind there be—is one that you
Alone, almost, of yours have had a wish
To contemplate. Therefore I call you friend,
And for reward offend you. For your saint,
Your saviour—I can only let him go,
And pray that he go far."

                    "I'm not so racked
And clubbed that I need that," Bartholow said.
"When you berate yourself the most, your words
Contrive to fall on me; and when I feel them,
As now I do, undoubtedly I deserve them.
Yet I'm aware of an unconsciousness
Of their importance when this friend of mine,
Who saved me, and then made me wish him dead,
Inspires them. There is much you do not know
Of doors that are within us and are closed
Until one comes who has the key to them.
I have no proof that one to open them
Need be infallible. If he be sincere,
And have within himself the mastery . . .
I don't know.   All I know is, it was done.
There were no mummeries, no miracles;
There was no degradation of the wits,
Or of the will; there was no name for it;
Yet something in me opened and the light
Came in. I could have given him all but life
For recompense. Also, I could have killed him,
Indifferently, while he was on the floor,
And I was at his throat."

           "Go on from there,"
Said Umfraville. "Go on again from there!"
A griffin grinning into a smooth pool
Would have seen something like the face just then
That beamed on Bartholow, who dried his forehead
Mechanically with his handkerchief,
And sighed—and after, in a wan way, smiled.
"Go on from there, and—well, *aderitque Apollo;*
And he will give your language golden wings.
Your theme inveigles me," pursued the griffin.

"No I shall not go on again from there,"
Bartholow said, and frowned remorsefully.
"For long before I struck him I could see—
As I see now. And it was he who did it—
Who gave me sight. Was I blind when I struck him?
If I was blind a moment, I was blind.
He said that I was aboriginal,
But I'll say I was blind. I would have killed him,
Certainly. But I would not kill him now,
Nor would I wish him ill. We must all pay,
Somehow; and I believe that he has paid.
If he has not, he must. And as for her—

Your way for her may be as well as any.
If you say she was dead before she died,
She may have been so; and I may have killed her—
Before she died. I had not thought of that.
The way of custom is the way of death,
Or may be so, for some who follow it
Too far; and so it was I may have killed her.
I do not ask of you that you say now
Whether I did or not. You do not know.
She married without love; and when love came,
A life too late, I should have been a liar
To take it, or to say I treasured it;
For when it came at last, out of the ruins,
It was one remnant more among too many;
It was love only as a beauty scarred
Is beauty still. I could forgive the scar,
For that was nothing, and was far behind me;
But with him in the house I could not say so.
It was the smear on him that made me blind,
And made me strike. I do not know him yet.
Only, I know that I can see again,
With a new sight,—and that he made me see.
Strange bottles, if you will."

"Damnably strange—
And effervescent," grunted Umfraville.
"The wine in this one blew the stopper out,
And yet the wine stays good. It's not the rule.
Well, you are out for knowledge, or for wisdom,
And wisdom has a driving way with rules.
Your wine may be the best; though for myself,
Give me the old elixir that you gave me
That morning when I brought the noble fish.
You do not know him yet? You never will.
So let him fade."

                    "I cannot make him fade,
Though I could make him go." Bartholow felt
Again the sweat of effort on his forehead,
But otherwise, though more pallid, was himself,
And had himself in hand. "Now I'll go home,
He said. "And I shall find her waiting there.
No, he will not be there. And if he were——"

"He would amerce you for your negligence,
And you'd requite him with another cheque.
You must go farther for the mystery
Than that, if you're to find out where it lives.

Wherever he may be now, at your expense,
Whatever he may have done to you, or for you,
I seem to hear him laughing.   I'm a sinner
To say it, but I say it for your safety,
Not for my satisfaction.   As you know,
I have a speech that would be unbecoming
In anyone more inured and more at home
To the congealed amenities.   I'm a student,
Wherefore I see him laughing. . . . What the devil?
What is it?   What's the matter!"

Bartholow breathed
A little harder and a little faster
But had no power to speak till finally
The tension broke within him and his head
Fell forward like a stone into his hands;
And there, while memory clutched and humbled him,
He moaned and choked and laughed.   When he could
    speak,
His voice rocked with his body: "No—you don't!
You do not hear him laughing—for he wept!
I told him his obscure appearances
Could not be too obscure—and then, he wept!

[173]

I said he was a blackguard—and he wept!
He got a thousand dollars to get out—
And then he wouldn't go until he wept. . . .
Damn him, he wept!" He swayed there in his chair,
And all but out of it, laughing and moaning;
" 'I do not ask you for your gratitude,'
He said to me. He said that to me twice—
And then he wept! . . . And then they came to tell
What they had seen. They came up from the river—
In the moonlight . . . Strange bottles . . . Oh, my God!"

For a long time he sat there, trembling, shaking,
While Umfraville stood watching over him,
At first alarmed, at last assured. He waited,
Gravely and patiently, for another word
That would be slow, as he foresaw, to come;
But he still waited there, and still he waited,
With a fidelity inexhaustible
And a solemnity unchangeable,
Till questions that would not be answered yet
Glimmered a little in his doubtful eyes,
And over his amorphous countenance
There crept a slow and melancholy smile.

[174]

VIII

THERE was a wall of crimson all along
      The river now; and Bartholow, gazing at it,
Knew in his heart it was for the last time
That he was seeing those trees, and the still water,
Which he had known from childhood. In his house,
Or one that all his life had been his house,
Nothing of his remained that would be there
Tomorrow. In his heart nothing remained
But a recurrent ache when he remembered,
As now he must; for there would soon be sunset,
And he would soon be gone. He looked away
Over the falling lawn before him there
Where summer now lay buried and the first
Red leaves of autumn, flying silently,
Became a scattered silence on the grass.
He gazed, and saw the water through the rift
His axe had made that morning in the spring,

With Gabrielle watching him. That was long ago—
Too long, he told himself, to be seen there
Among so many pictures that were fading,
But were not yet invisible. No, not yet.
The frown of an unwelcome recollection
Wrinkled his face and changed it while he saw
The picture of a shipwreck on the air
Before him, and three faces. One was his,
That would be seen again; and one was hers,
That would not, surely, come back there again,
If even it might, to see or to be seen;
And there was one that he should see no more,
Living or dead, if life and death were kind.

Considering thus the scene that he had limned
Of cloudy and tempestuous memories,
He felt an echo sounding over floors
Of the old house—dismantled, empty, sold,
And waiting for new faces to come in
When he should go. "I shall be gone tomorrow,"
He thought; "and when this house where I was born
Has been here for another hundred years,
No doubt some unborn stranger will be gazing

[176]

As I am, at the river there below him,
With memories that may then be quite as cloudy
For him as mine have been for me today.
By then he may have lost as much as I
Lost once—or more, if there be more for one
To lose,—and he may then have found far less.
I wonder what a learned fisherman
Would say to that," he asked, as Umfraville,
After an exploration, came outside.
Tramping the flags with hard and heavy feet
He came to Bartholow as an animal,
Quaintly arrayed as man, might have approached
A master that he knew was leaving him.
There was a melancholy questioning
About him, and almost a dignity.
"They have left nothing that was made for me,
And that's as well," he said. "The books you sent
Will be enough, and I shall not forget
The man who sent them. That's my way of saying
All that I cannot say. And you said something?"

"I wondered if another hundred years
May find another tenant in this house

[177]

With memories that will be no merrier then
For him than mine are now for me. That's fancy,
As you would say. Too much in order, surely,
To be imagination, I should say."

"Merry is not your word this afternoon—
That's more what I should say," said Umfraville;
"Though I'll imagine a man somewhat merry,
Even in a tomb, alone there with his fathers,
If he be sure that one man, and one only,
Be not somewhere there with him. Your Penn-Raven,
Whether or not he's in your tomb, is not
Here in this house. At least, I didn't find him.
I'm wondering where three months have hidden him,
And how far off he is,—but I'm not asking.
If only we select our distances,
The world is of a comfortable size
For two to live in. What are you going to do,
If, as you may, sometime you come together,
And he weeps on your bosom for more gold?"

"We shall not come together," Bartholow said,
Smiling impassively. "And if we should,
We shall agree upon our distances.

[178]

He has instructions, and he has a mind
That's apt and adequate for their absorption.
Yes, I believe him.   Yes, and in his word."

"He has a mind, and he has more than that,"
The scholar growled at length, unwillingly,
"If all you say is true; and your condition
Would argue rather more for you than lies.
He says you are yourself; and if your look
Be the certificate of your quality,
You are not far from where he says you are.
On your report he says enough to sink
A shipload of the uninitiated.
He says if in considering what we are
We ponder for a season on the many
Behind us who have made us what we are,
Our vanity will hardly have an eyelash
To cling with to the ridge of our achievement;
He tells you those who struggle with more knots
Than yours have ever been would be themselves
A commonwealth—and that's all true enough;
He tells you that some evils are themselves
Their proper remedies—and that may pass;

[179]

He says the fruit that he has given to you
Is one you may not share with other men—
Though you may give it, and those getting it
May thrive on it, not knowing the name of it,
Or whence it comes to them, or wherefore.   Well,
I'm not so much at home there, but no matter.
He says that from now on you'll be alone,
Wherever you find yourself, and that you'll carry
Whatever it is you call it with you always,
Whether you will or not.   He says, also,
There was a man, meaning himself—oh, damn him—
That was already on his way to save you,
Knowing no more, it seems, of your existence
Than you knew there was anywhere after you
A thing like him.   And there you are.   Joy! Joy!
If I were but a hand-step nearer bedlam,
I'd half believe the blackguard was half right."

"I called him once a blackguard—to his face,"
Bartholow said, reflecting; "and I met
With no denial.   Yet I could wonder now
Just what the silence he commanded then

Was made of. Partly sorrow, I am sure,—
And I forgive your smiling; partly pain;
Partly compassionate bewilderment—
And I forgive your laughing. I should laugh,
Undoubtedly, or wish to, in your place;
If I were in your place, I'd be as blind
As you are, and as much to be forgiven.
Excused, I mean. If we're too soft with nature
In our forgivings, nature may laugh at us
As you were laughing then, and fling them back
Like vitriol in our faces. I'll excuse
Your mirth, my learned friend, but don't do that;
For now, to make it worse, you are too solemn—
As if you feared that you had wounded me.
You have not wounded me. Do you remember
That morning when I knocked you out of bed
So early—when I told you it had happened
And went somewhat to pieces at the end?
There was a time when I too should have laughed
At the mere whispered probability
Of such a scene awaiting anyone
Assisting at my drama. But you waited,
And in your wisdom never said a word,

[181]

Or laughed. You might as well have laughed at that
As at compassionate bewilderment—
Or what it was Penn-Raven may have felt
For me when he was told he was a blackguard—
Which, in the compound of his opposites,
I'll say to you he has. Now you look better.
If you have not forgotten such a morning,
You may remember that I mentioned then
Some doors within us that may not be opened
Till one may come who has the key to them.
When he has opened them and has made free
The life within that was a prisoner there,
How is a man who has a door in him
Still closed, like yours, to say what else he was
Than blackguard? Even though I may say my doors
Are open, I'm not saying what else he was,
Or why it is that nature baits for men,
Between them and the pit, so many traps
To save them with a poisoned obligation.
Nature has ways, you say, not reasons. Well,
They lead us, if we find and follow them,
Strangely away from death."

"And into it—
As often, or as likely." Umfraville
Stared with a brooding melancholy scowl
Over the flaming trees and into time
Behind him, but he found so little there
That he soon looked again at Bartholow,
And with constrained inquiry. "Quite as often,"
He said, "or quite as likely. And for that,
If you've an urging in you, going forward,
To stray back by the phantom-ridden **ways**
Of memory—*tout' aniarotaton.*
Your steps are elsewhere. Pindar said all that,
You may remember,—*nessun maggior*
Dolore—long before there was a Dante.
You find it also in Cimmerian,
If you look far enough. But what's it all
To me? I'm asking—what's it all to me?
I'm only a dry mummy among books,
Except when I'm a-fishing or I'm drinking.
For me there's nothing wholly bad that's old,
And nothing good that's new since Porson type.
While time has a digamma left in it
For bait, I'll set my trap and catch myself.

Your traps and ways are yours; though as for poison,
Leaving him out, I pray that by this time
You see at last where custom was at work
Before he came. You fancied once I told you
That you had killed her,—which was nothing more
Than a politeness to Melpomene
On your part, and a negligence on mine.
My fault again," he added, having watched
A cloud across the face of Bartholow:
'I should have put more clothes upon my words;
I should have said it without saying it;
I should have said, 'For God's sake, my good friend,
Relinquish all such dutiful self-damnation
As that. There were you two in the dark together,
And there her story ends.' The leaves you turn
Are blank; and where a story ends, it ends.
The author may have lost enthusiasm,
Or changed his mind, and so may write another—
But not upon those leaves. Books are my life,
And when there is no more of one, I know it.
'Let me be worthy of your mysteries'—
Or, at the least, of this one. Say to custom
All I have said to you, and then forget."

Bartholow, gazing at the open door,
Could half believe that he saw there the ghost
Of Gabrielle, going in and vanishing,
Slowly, as he had seen her when she left him,
That morning in the spring, when he had said
So much to her about a phantom house,
Which he knew as well then must always be
A phantom as he knew it was one now.
Before it was all gone the vision turned
Upon him the once unrevealing eyes
That now revealed so much; for he could see
All that he did not see when she was there,
A woman and alive. But he saw nothing
That would have been as happy in his house
Unbuilt as in her grave where she was lying.

He shook his head slowly at Umfraville.
"No, I shall not wear out the time that's left
In poring always over those blank leaves,"
He said; "and maybe they are not so blank
To me this afternoon as once they were.
There may be nothing on them for your eyes,

[185]

Which in their turn see much that might as well
Be blank for mine. I shall remember always
Your counsel, and should always value it,
Being yours, whether or not I followed it.
Your Custom, undeniably a giant,
Is not so monstrous that, if we had vision
To see ourselves before it was too late,
We might not overthrow him for another;
For we must have our giants, though the pride
Of our inferiority may insist
That we disguise them. There are more at work
On a forlorn disguise to fit the old
Than on a proper garment for the new.
New giants are at first intolerably
Not ours, and are uncoverably naked."

"If you can see all that," said Umfraville,
"There are no pits of memory behind you
That you need waste a fear on, or a sigh.
Go out into your world and be a tailor,
But leave my world with me. I'll stay in it
With my familiar giants, who are dead,
And therefore do no harm."

Bartholow smiled:
"About what time were they annihilated—
These harmless giants of yours? They are not dead,
My friend, though some of them are overthrown;
And even tonight, if you bestir yourself,
There may be time enough, and a way made,
For you to go with me—as far, at least,
As where your giants reigned." He looked again,
Affectionately, at an asking face
That hardly was a face, and read upon it
A loneliness of long deformity
That was the lonelier somehow for its learning.
"An hour or two on the Acropolis
Would let you see how far they are from dead."

The scholar shook his head: "They are not there;
And you are wronging them and wronging me,
Saying they are alive. They are all dead,
And I would have them so. No, I'll stay here.
Here I shall have my own Acropolis,
And have it as I will. If I were there,
All I should see would be the scraps and ashes
Of a lost world that I shall have intact,

And uninfested with modernities,
If I stay here.   And if I went with you,
For God's sake what would you be doing with me?
Men would be saying soon to one another
That you were Satan, going to and fro
In the earth again and up and down in it,
With me along with you to scare away
The curious, who might otherwise be annoying.
No, no!   There is a best place in the world
For me; and that's as far as possible
From your activities.   You are going to live,
At last, that more may live.   It is all true—
All as your prophet, damn him, said it was.
I see it now, but there was a long time
When I saw nothing but that meaty-faced,
Fanatic, esoteric head of his.
Nature, that has a deal to answer for,
Put something in him, inadvertently,
Prepared and graduated for the lymph
And essence of a worthier organism.
That's how it must have been.   If you say not,
You say it on the same authority
That I say I'm a fairy of the hills.

No, no,—the place for me is over there
Across the river. There among my dead,
And only there, I'm properly alive.
So there I'll go, and with no more ado.
You dine tonight with friends who are concerned
That you have sold unwisely and too soon—
And then you go. You are the only friend
That I have left; and if that's not so bad
As a bad name to take away with you,
Shelve it among your memories. Good-bye!"

Bartholow pressed his hand and held it long
Before he let it go again. "Good-bye!"
He said. "We should have known each other better
If I had known myself. A word of yours
Will always find me—somewhere. You know best
Where you belong—whether among your dead,
Who are still with us, or among the living
Who are not yet alive."

          The man of books
Answered him only with a lonely smile;
And then, among the slowly falling leaves,
He walked away and vanished gradually,

Like one who had not been. Yet he had been
For Bartholow the man who knew him best,
And loved him best,—acknowledging always one
That had betrayed and saved him. He was gone,
Also, and there was no more to be said
Of him; and there was no more to be paid,
Apparently, on either side. The sum
Of all that each had ever owed the other
Was covered, sealed, and cancelled in a grave,
Where lay a woman doomed never to live—
That he who had adored her and outgrown her
Might yet achieve. He sighed, and saw the ivy
Glimmering on the wall of the old house
Like an old garment over covered years,
Till his imagination made of it
The cover and the integument itself
Of the unseen. The tangled roots of wrong
Were drawing always out of hidden soil
The weird existence of a tangled vine
Too vaguely intertwisted and involved
For sanguine gardeners, who might only prune
Or train a few new branches. "Well, that's something,"
Gabrielle might have answered then, he fancied;

And she might then have smiled as wearily
As on that unforgotten unreal evening
When she had touched his forehead with her lips
Before she had gone silently upstairs,
And silently away. . . .

    He locked the door,
Aware that even the key to the old house
That had so long been his was his no longer,
And in the twilight went away from there.
Over the footworn flagstones and the gravel,
Under the trees and over the long road
Between him and the gate, he walked away,
Knowing that he had seen for the last time
The changeless outline of those eastern hills,
And all those changing trees that flamed along
A river that should flow for him no more.